When They Invite You
to Dinner — Eat First

When They Invite You to Dinner — Eat First

Laurie Burns Hennicker
and Marshall Masters

YOUR OWN WORLD BOOKS
yowbooks.com

Laurie "Burnsey" Hennicker
In Loving Memory

Copyright

First Yowbooks Edition 2004

Paperback
ISBN: 0-9755177-8-3
dx.doi.org/10.1572/0975517783

Adobe eBook
ISBN: 0-9755177-9-1
dx.doi.org/10.1572/0975517791

Microsoft eBook
ISBN: 0-9755177-5-9
dx.doi.org/10.1572/0975517759

Mobipocket eBook
ISBN: 1-59772-003-8
dx.doi.org/10.1572/1597720038

Palm eBook
ISBN: 1-59772-004-6
dx.doi.org/10.1572/1597720046

YOUR OWN WORLD BOOKS
an imprint of Your Own World, Inc.
Carson City, NV USA
yowbooks.com
SAN: 256-1646

"A man must never make
his wife weep, for God
counts her every tear."

– *Morris Burns (Papa)*

Table of Contents

Welcome to the Family

Today, depression means it is time to take a pill, instead of a taking the day off with the family.. Have you considered that people are referred to as that when it used to be who? The endearing warmth of mamma and papa have given way to the more economical mom and dad.

I grew up as an only child in the Great Depression. During that time I had no idea that my parents were different from the average mamma and papa. Everything I did was praised; however I looked, I was told I was beautiful; if something broke it was good luck; if it rained it was time to play hooky; and if there was a hurt, it was time to divert attention elsewhere.

All of my life, my friends have come to me with their problems, and I always had a My Mamma Used to Say story. I have never been at a loss for some example that I could give to ease a burden, or make an occasion more of an occasion for friends and family. And when life was a burden for me, they'd give the stories right back with love.

Come meet my family of the Great Depression years and share our love and laughter.

MEET PAPA (Morris)

Papa had many sides, including Moses the Lawgiver, the Judge, the Mediator, Samson, and some names Mamma called him on certain occasions. Papa was twenty-six years older than Mamma.

Papa had silver hair and beard, and sparkling brown eyes. He was a scholar and I never remember hearing him raise his voice. He came to this great country from Russia, and his love for America was like a daily prayer of thankfulness.

MEET MAMMA (Rose)

Mamma came here from Austria. She was tiny, with flaxen gold hair and blue, blue eyes. She stood 4 feet 11 inches, and I always remember her as Humpty Dumpty on chicken legs. Her complexion was exquisite. Mamma was like a bubbling spark of rainbow electricity: every movement, every gesture, even her speech revealed that she was a complete show in herself.

One of my fondest childhood memories was the simple act of mailing a letter with Mamma. She used to walk me down to the mailbox to mail a letter, lift me up, and tell me to scream into the box two or three times with directions.

ME? (Laurie): I was born in Harlem Hospital, Manhattan, on November 5, 1917. When Papa saw me, he said to Mamma: Rose, we don't have a child—we have an angel. I always tried to be their angel. I have no regrets and can think of nothing I should have done differently.

More About Laurie

I am Marshall Masters, the proud son of Laurie Burns Hennicker (1917–1998). She was not only an intelligent woman but she was also a truly liberated woman long before there was a movement for equality.

Her doctor once told me with an affectionate grin, "Your mother is the only person I know who does not have an ego problem. I suppose it goes back to her childhood." The doctor got it right. It did.

My mother grew up as an only child in the middle of the Great Depression, in the Lower East Side of New York. She was born to a wise, educated father, a tzaddik (spiritual leader) who wrote plays for the Yiddish theatre, and a mother who spoke five languages. How do I know this? It took years of coaxing to get her to tell me what her life was really like back then. This is because mom never liked to talk about the Great Depression in terms of suffering. In the mornings, as a young girl, she would heat the coal stove and iron her only school uniform to look smart for school. "Sure it was rough, but that's life," mom would often say. We were mostly broke, but never poor. You take life where you find it."

So rather than dwell on how many families had to share the same toilet, mom relished her childhood memories of having a piano in the home and how she felt loved each day. To her, the term Great Depression meant the joy of living in unconditional love.

When America entered World War II, mom immediately decided to enlist in the Women's Marine Corps. However, her physical revealed that she was pregnant. In those days, that was the end of that. Undeterred from her personal mission to be a part of the war effort, she went to work for the British Intelligence office in New York—not because she was pregnant, but because she happened to be the fastest typist in New York at the time.

For the British, she was the ideal candidate for a special job because she could type faster than the Teletype machines of the day. Consequently, she operated the Teletype machines used to transmit vital meeting point messages to the freighters and English warships that plied the U-boat infested waters of the Atlantic, and she often knew about troop movements even before Prime Minister Winston Churchill did. She did other things as well, but her lips always remained sealed. Of course, this would drive me to distraction. Especially after seeing a new James Bond movie.

After the war, mom was the vice president of the Green Kriegsman Paper Company, the largest newsprint paper distributor in the United States. Following that, she became the general manager for Jaguar motors in the United States, working for Hofmann Motor Car Company until she moved from the East Coast to the West Coast in 1950, and finally settled in Phoenix, Arizona.

In the 1970s, mom became an empty nester and decided that she would go back to college. She enjoyed it so much, she became a professional student and earned eight bachelor degrees from Arizona State University.

She had very few regrets in life, and one of them had been her missed opportunity to enlist in the Marines during of WWII. So, she enrolled in the ROTC and rose to the rank of major, as the department's Public Information Officer. All of us in the family were proud of mom. She was in her 50s and the oldest cadet in the country to complete all four years of Army ROTC training.

I happened to be going to ASU at the same time and was also a medic in the Arizona Army National Guard. When the guys in my guard unit found out about her through a local newspaper article, they started ribbing me about that the fact that my mother actually did wear combat boots.

Truth be known, it didn't bother me. Mom and I had a working deal. I'd spit shine her combat boots and in return, she'd type my English papers for me. It was a marvelous arrangement to say the least. She had shiny boots and I had English papers that shined.

A notable event for mom happened during an ROTC war game maneuver in the field. After being captured, she flipped the whole deal around by capturing the opposing force platoon that had taken her prisoner, using a hidden rat-tail comb.

The opposing force platoon leader complained, "Yah, we should have followed procedure and checked her, but how do you frisk someone old enough to be your grandmother?" The war game judges didn't buy it and from then on, younger students in the ROTC program at ASU would often say, If Laurie can do it, so can you!

A true patriot, were she alive today, I believe she would heartily agree with the views of General Tommy Franks. During a recent magazine interview he noted that 9-11 had left an indelible "crease" in American history, and he is right.

Since that tragic day, we Americans have become a little less self-preoccupied as a people, and along the way, we've begun the process of reaffirming the importance of family for our own happiness as well as for the security of our nation. These are the traditional values that pulled my mother's generation through a depression and a world war.

As we now watch the threat levels move up and down through the color bars, we can only wonder when there will be another man-made or natural disaster to overcome. While keeping stockpiles of food, medicines, and blankets on hand is both prudent and wise, in the end, it will be our unconditional love for one another that will give us the spiritual strength to endure and rebuild. Or in the words of my mother: Money lost, nothing lost. Hope lost, all is lost. It was from her parents that my mother learned these vital and simple rules of survival.

If, by chance, I were offered the opportunity to go back in time for a brief visit, I would want to go back to meet my maternal grandparents. Especially grandfather Morris. Although I never had the opportunity to look into his eyes, I have loved his soul all my life thanks to my mother's wonderful childhood stories, which I now have the privilege of sharing with you in this uplifting book.

Grandfather Morris was from Russia, and in that part of the world there was an old saying: "Life is like a zebra: one day black, one day white. And it always changes."

During the white stripes of my life, these stories were always a wonderful way for me to share love and laughter.

And when those inevitable black stripes came along (as they always do), these very same stories helped me to pull through. Again, Money lost, nothing lost. Hope lost, all is lost.

With this in mind…

Is your life going through a white stripe right now? Read this book, and share in the joy that comes from unconditional love.

Is your life going through a black stripe right now? Read this book, and share in the nourishment of unconditional love.

God bless you, and may we all live in peace with hope, joy, and unconditional love.

The Goose of Peace

When Mamma started to scream for me to get her bundle of keys, I knew she was going to have a fight with Papa and throw them at him. I ran to get the keys and gave them to Mamma and then stood back waiting for the instructions I knew Mamma would give me very quickly.

It didn't matter what the fight was about. Mamma would usually say, You're a schmuck, then throw the keys. Papa would simply catch them and throw them back gently and say, Here, Rose, try again. Mamma usually did, and then she would turn and all 4 feet 11 inches of her would storm into the bedroom.

There, Mamma grabbed a suitcase and, opening all of Papa's drawers and sometimes even her own, she dumped everything into the suitcase, closed it, and came back out. Papa and I just stood there because we both knew to wait for Mamma's cues.

Mamma marched over to the door, threw it open, set the suitcase outside, and then planted herself. Then she threw her right arm out and, head high, just said OUT. '

Papa went out, and Mamma slammed the door shut so hard that Papa had to screw the hinges back the next day.

Then, she immediately turned with excitement and sparkling eyes and said, Well, hurry up, let's go—get out the roasting pan, turn the oven on to 375 degrees, set the table. Hurry, hurry or we will miss the show!

We had everything ready and after what seemed like an eternity, came a gentle knock on the door. Mamma ran to the door, opened it just enough to permit Papa's arm into the room, and from his fist there hung a goose: plucked, cleaned, and ready to join the onions and beets in the roaster.

Mamma grabbed the goose, stuck it in the pan, and into the oven it went.

Mamma headed for the bathtub with me by the hand so we could get bathed and be ready for dinner and the show.

Papa just picked up his suitcase in the hall where he had left it. Humming, he went into the bedroom and unpacked. We all dressed and ate, and then went to the movies.

Everyone has his own Goose of Peace. For me it was homemade Italian ravioli which my husband and kids knew I couldn't resist regardless of how furious I was.

Have a goose...your own way.

The More Expensive the Damage,
the Greater the Luck

Mamma had a cut glass bowl which she treasured because it was Aunt Helen's, may she rest in peace, who brought it from Europe.

I broke it, accidentally, while washing it and it smashed into a million diamonds all over the sink and floor. Mamma ran into the kitchen and saw what happened. She immediately grabbed me and started to dance and sing, Whatever evil spirits were to have befallen us, have vanished with the broken bowl. Aunt Helen is still looking after us! The more expensive or precious a piece was, the greater the joy when it broke, for the greater the evil that would have befallen us.

My daughter and her little friends were washing my cut glass like Mamma had taught me: fill half the sink with hot soap water and the other half of the sink with boiling hot water and some bluing to make the glass sparkle; set the cut glass on a Turkish towel laid out beforehand. My daughter was explaining about the history of this piece and that, when the compote dish slipped out of her soapy hands, and shattered. All her little friends gasped and froze, and then stood in amazed disbelief when I took her in my arms, and we started to dance and chant. We invited the other girls into the circle and they got the hang of it quickly. We had a marvelously good time and were so relieved to know that unforeseen troubles would not come.

Then I explained to them, as my mother to me, that if it is an accident, this is what we do. If it is carelessness, we scream, just like any other mother.

Carelessness we must learn from, but accidents happen to everyone, and guilt should never be attached to them..

Gee, did we lose a lot of cut glass and gain a lot of laughs.

My Kid's a Genius — You're the Dope

When I got an A, I was a genius; when I got a B, the teacher was a dope. That was Mamma's philosophy and she lived by it

When I was a kid, most of the teachers were old maids and cranky. One term I got a dandy who made me her pet grievance in life. She referred to me as the little fat Jew, and she found a nice way to punish me. We used to wear white middy blouses with sailor collars, and the cloth was as heavy as jeans. One of my middy blouses had torn, and you had to place your order and wait for another. This teacher knew that I had only the one blouse. This was her opportunity. Your blouse is dirty, she said, go home and change it. I tried to explain that I could not get the ink off the collar, which I'd gotten because the boy behind me kept dunking my curls in the inkwell on his desk. It didn't matter. I had to go home, in the snow, crying all the way. Why? Because every night I washed the middy blouse. Every morning I got up early, but still after Mamma and Papa who left for the store at six o'clock.

I washed the blouse in ice cold faucet water. I lit the coal stove and set the irons on to heat. I laid a folded sheet on the kitchen table and ironed the blouse.

I did not dare to put my coat on, because the blouse was still damp and almost wet around the seams and the sailor collar. I ran all the way back to school with my coat in my arms. By the time I got to class, I was starched. The blouse had frozen on me. The teacher said nothing, and I took my seat.

The next day we had a test, and we passed our papers to the front to be corrected. They were graded by the teacher, and returned to us. The test was finished. I got the usual 100 percent. I bent down to tie my shoelaces, and my teacher took my test paper out of the bundle, tore it up, and gave me a zero for the day.

I was always afraid to cry because Mamma might see my red eyes and beat the heck out of whoever caused me to cry. Now I couldn't hold back my tears anymore. I cried all day, on the way home, and until Mamma came home. You see, my report card would show a lower average because of the zero, and Mamma would want to know why. Well, I told her now not about the blouse incidents which kept repeating but did not affect my grade, but about the test paper. I had not folded my hands on the desk and sat up erect, but had bent to tie my shoes.

I was numb with worry because I knew Mamma would not let it pass. Her genius got 100 percent and no dope would take it away from her. About ten o'clock the next morning, the door smashed open: all 4 feet 11 inches of Mamma took two steps into the classroom, stopped to spot me, then fixing her eyes on me, nodded her head toward the teacher. I had to nod back, signaling to Mamma that yes, she was the one who gave me the zero.

Before the teacher could turn and be sickly sweet to a parent, Mamma was on top of her. The teacher was about a head taller and fifty pounds heavier than Mamma. I didn't worry about Mamma, I was sorry for the teacher.

First, Mamma pulled the hairpins out of her hair so Mamma could get a good grip on the head. While one hand was handling the hairpins, the other hand was ripping the beautiful georgette blouse to ribbons. When Mamma could get a grip on the hair where it was long, she got another grip on the hair where it was short, and brought the two parts of the body together, adding her knees for extra whacks.

The teacher finally broke loose and ran down the hall screaming toward the principal's office. Boy, was I scared. Mamma just grabbed me by the hand and said, Come. As we marched out of the classroom, all I could think about what was what my teacher would do to me after all this.

When we got to the principal's office, Mamma could see the teacher through the open door and began to take after her again screaming, I'll teach you to give my daughter a zero—you dope you—you should be teaching in a toilet, not in a school!

The principal came out into her waiting room and Mamma stopped, as she quickly escorted the teacher out through another door. She then showed Mamma into her office, where she remained for what seemed like the longest time to me. Then, I began to hear them both screaming with laughter. Gee, I thought, Mamma is telling jokes and here I am in trouble for life.

The inner door finally opened, and I could see the principal making gestures with her hands to indicate the size of the teacher and the size of Mamma, and in between she clutched her sides laughing. I got transferred to another class and finished the term without any problems, and with my A.

The very next term who do I get? Yup, the go-home-and-wash-your-middy-blouse old maid. I trembled. I tried to transfer out of her class, even out of the school. But I was stuck in her class.

Guess what? She had MARRIED. Now she loved the world, kids in general, and the little fat Jew in particular, and I spent almost that whole term sitting on her lap in front of the class while she played with my curls.

Gee, I would rather have run home to wash the middy blouse, than to have the kids rib me. They quit when I found I could bribe them not to taunt me—because guess who was the monitor capable of handing out A's? You bet. Teacher's pet: me.

I think all old maid teachers should get married.

Love Is Not What You Say, But...

Mamma and Papa belonged to a benevolent society, usually organized by people who came from the same town in Europe. Money was raised through dues, which were $6.00 per couple per year, and through theater and dinner banquets. I was usually the only child present, because Mamma and Papa took me everywhere they went. I remember the excitement of new clothes, and also remember how Papa threw me over his shoulder when it was time to go home.

At one of the banquets, someone asked me whether I spoke any foreign languages. I answered that I spoke eight languages. They wanted me to say something. In all eight? I questioned. Yes, was the reply.

Well, I set my feet apart, put my hands on my hips, inclined my head, and with a twinkle in my eyes spun off phrases in eight different languages. As I spoke each one, more people joined, and the laughter got louder and louder, but I did not see Mamma get madder and madder.

Usually when we got home, Papa dumped me into bed and other than removing my shoes, I was permitted to just sleep through the night.

Not this night.

This night, Mamma had Papa dump me into a hard wooden chair, and while I was still half asleep, I came to life very quickly when I heard Mamma say she was going to wash my mouth out with Octagon, this horrible brown soap. Boy, I remembered when my cousin did that to me, so I opened my eyes wide and listened.

But, Rose, Papa was saying, the kid didn't know what she was saying. '

What do you mean she didn't know, Mamma said, she said it, and everyone else knew.

The argument went back and forth, with Mamma running back and forth to find the horrible brown soap.

Then Mamma turned to me and said, Well, what do you think you were saying in eight languages?

I love you, I said.

I love you! ' Mamma screamed, where did you get that from?

Well, Mamma, every time Papa goes by you he pinches you or your bushy, and you always look at him with a twinkle and say one of those things.

Papa was convulsed with laughter. Mamma didn't want me to see her laugh, and sent me to bed. I was just happy that I didn't get the Octagon treatment. As I was leaving, I heard Papa say to Mamma, See Rose, when you say 'kiss my ass' in eight languages, even the kid knows you love me.

If a Little Is Good, a Lot Is Better

I was about nine years old and had developed a nonstop appetite for frankfurters. Suddenly one day, I began to itch all over. I was busier than a dog with fleas. The doctor diagnosed it as frankfurter itis and prescribed castor oil.

For ten cents, the druggist would fill a water glass with castor oil, and Mamma thought I should drink the whole glass. Just knowing what it was made me gag, and I refused. Mamma got out the broom and started chasing me around the room. I wound up cornered on the bed and was almost enjoying the action. Every time I jumped, Mamma swept the broom under me. I loved jump rope, and was enjoying this bedspring trampoline action and the broom jump.

Papa watched for awhile, then he suggested that Mamma leave the room and he would deal with me. She had no alternative. Papa said, Go get me some bread in the kitchen. I did.

Now Papa pulled out a fresh white towel and set the glass of castor oil and the bread on it. He broke off small pieces of bread, dipped each in the castor oil and ate, licking his fingers. Now, not even in Russia did we have such wonderful oil, he said.

If Papa was enjoying this awful oil so much, what was I missing? After all, I didn't think to question Papa, because once after a doctor had prescribed medicine for him to be taken one teaspoon every four hours, I watched papa uncap the bottle and drink the whole thing in one gulp. But Papa, I said, the doctor said you have to take a teaspoon every four hours. '

Foolish child, Papa responded, why should I be sick for forty-eight hours by taking a teaspoon? If a little is good, a lot is better, and I am already cured.

Challenge and the Underdog

There are no spoiled children. Love does not spoil, it aids in the ripening process and thrives on laughter. Sad children, through neglect, abuse, or misunderstanding, appear to be spoiled, but it is only that they are lost.

More than ever today we need hope in this hopeless, scientific world. The happiness of childhood and the strengths gained in happiness are what carry you through adulthood. Each year, we cut the span of childhood shorter.

You will have enough time for seriousness when you are grown, so enjoy your childhood, Papa and Mamma taught me.

Challenge lived in our home. Challenge was not competition, nor was it rivalry. In our home it meant sharpening the teeth of your mind on each other. Learning was questioning and responding. My favorite was Papa's test for my friends.

In the olden days, men would wander from town to town bringing news to friends and relatives. They would be fed for the news. They were beggars performing a service. The law required that the hungry be fed, and especially on the Sabbath. However, there was an exception: If feeding the hungry meant depriving your own, you must not do so.

Now knowing this, here is the test: It is the Sabbath, and there is a knock on the door. You open the door and find two men standing there, begging a meal. You have a wife and six children. You figure if you take a little bit from each of the eight plates, you can make one more and hurt none. You can feed only one, therefore you must choose, so you ask why they beg.

One says he was orphaned before he was two years old. He never had an opportunity to learn a trade or go to school, and had become a beggar in his youth.

The other man says he had been a rich businessman, but through mischance and misjudgment, he had gone broke and had to resort to being a beggar.

Which one would you feed and why? In America, we are taught to love the underdog, and to feel pity for him. The answer I get from adults I try this on is the man who had been orphaned and they cannot explain why.

The answer Papa gave was this: You must feed the man who was once rich. He knows shame, and if you refuse him, he will starve to death rather than beg. The beggar is accustomed to begging and knows no shame, and will simply keep knocking on doors until he gets his meal. If not, he is also accustomed to going without and can take it. And, if you help the man who once was on top, he will be on top again. The other will continue to be a beggar until death.

The choice of which one to feed is simple—the reason is important. Like in law, the decision must support the reasoning, and many times if you will reason something out you may come to a different decision than the one you felt positive about.

Reason is the seasoning for understanding.

Don't Hold Hands... You'll
Get Pregnant

I loved the Sabbath, which began with the first star on Friday night, and ended with the first star on Saturday night. On Friday, Mamma was always home. She cooked, and I cleaned and changed records on the Victrola. I loved Sousa, and played his records over and over; I also played Italian songs. I did not like Caruso when I was cleaning house because I couldn't dance to opera. The smells of Mamma's cooking were so good. Yeast and butter cakes, gefilte (stuffed) fish, and chicken soup all blended into a delicious aroma.

When the work was done, Mamma and I would take a bath together. Then it was Tootsie's turn —our poodle Tootsie was shown her Hershey bar, and she kept her eyes on it all though the bath knowing it was her treat for being good.

In the evening, the candles burning on the dining room table gave out the only light, and my friends would come. We would sit around reading books, eating Mamma's delicious ruggalach (little horn-shaped desserts filled with sugar, cinnamon, nuts, and raisins), and drinking cold, cold milk. Time for bed was signaled by the candles coming to a slow end.

On Saturday morning, it was my job to run to the bakery and get cheese Danish and the Forward, a Jewish newspaper. Then I would hop back into bed with Mamma and she would read to me.

Mamma's favorite was the Bintle Brief —or short story—so she would always read that first. I used to think it meant Bundle of Grief.

I remember one story about a young girl who did not wait to grow up. She did not listen to her mother, went out with boys and got pregnant. Worse yet, she never married. Then would come the tragic part, worse than her breaking her parents' hearts and ruining her own life—the worst part was the poor child, destined to be an outcast for life. We always cried, and then Mamma would take one of Papa's handkerchiefs, give her nose a hearty blow, and say, See, listen what I tell you. Never hold hands with a boy because that is how you get pregnant.

I never questioned Mamma's statements and advice. I never held hands with a boy until after I was married. I remember once, though, when a boy helped me across a big puddle and I held out my hand to him for help. He wrote me the most beautiful letter saying he felt like a prince helping a princess. But that was not really holding hands.

Decades later when my own daughter entered her teens, I wondered how to tell her about boys. What could I say? It was then that I decided to pass along Mamma's good advise: Never hold hands with a boy because that is how you get pregnant. Interestingly enough, I remember that I did not question my own mother about this bit of advice, and to my amazement, neither did my own daughter.

While enjoying a cup of coffee with a neighbor, I told her about this and she asked me to give her own daughter about boys her Mamma's advice. Unlike my daughter, her children did question me. So I—now in my forties—had to figure out what Mamma was trying to say.

I decided it was simply this: If you hold hands, the hands begin to creep up the arm, around the shoulder, down the front, etc. And it leads to children having fatherless children.

Sooooo...nowthat I knew what Mamma meant, and I added to it my own bit of advice: Don't start what you can't finish.

No matter when you're born and come of age, some things always make perfect sense. Mamma had it right the first time.

Rainy Hooky

Wake up, it's raining, Mom would say. Then she would feel my head and say, You're not feeling so good, and I knew I could turn over, go back to sleep, and not have to go to school.

God forbid I should really be sick—then I would have to go to school. Why? Because Mamma reasoned that when you go to school you forget you are sick, so staying home in bed was something you did, when you wanted to be doing something other than school that day.

I would get some extra sleep, just enough for me to miss school. Then Mamma would be back and shake me. So—why are you sleeping away the day? We have a lot to do. This meant dishes, dusting, and straightening just enough to make it look good. Then we were off.

First we went shopping. Then when the matinees started, we went to the movies where Mamma would catch a delicious nap.

I never dared to play hooky. Mamma took care of my hooky days, and it was my own obligation and duty to catch up with my studies and bring home the perpetual A which Mamma demanded from me, her genius. Except for Mamma's inclement weather days, I had a perfect attendance record, and if I was sick on a nice day, it was my own fault.

Gilly, Golly, Gooly

In 1976 our country celebrated its bicentennial. Ours was a country to which immigrants came and adapted themselves; now it is a country which adapts itself to its citizenry.

Come with me back to another year, another Saturday, when our country was trying out a new law called Prohibition and an old immigrant was trying out a new country called America: the land of Golden Opportunity.

Papa could not conceive of a Sabbath without wine for the Friday night blessing, and schnapps for the Saturday blessing. It was simple: if you could not buy it at the store, you made it—just like in Russia.

I remember Papa used to make something he called kvase, a carbonated drink much like champagne. In the spring, Papa rented a store, bottled the drink, and sold it to a fleet of young men who went out and sold it. I remember that some people in the bottling business offered Papa $50,000 for his kvase formula, and how excited Papa got. As soon as the men left, Papa grabbed Mamma and started to dance up and down singing Rose A Li—we've got it.!

Schmuck, said Mamma, I'll tell you what you've got—a good business. I said No. '

So, Papa never sold the formula; we never got any money for Papa to lose on another business, and Mamma was happy.

For the Sabbath schnapps, I remember Papa used all kinds of things like potatoes, prunes, and stale bread. For some reason, I did not help Papa make either the Schnapps or the kvase, but I did help make the wine, and have taught my children to do so. Papa had a partner in the wine business, but when his partner tried to water the wine, Papa walked out. Mamma always said that the only good partnership was that between a husband and a wife.

One Saturday evening, just as we were sitting down to the closing service at sundown, there was a knock at the door. Papa followed his religion and its philosophy which commanded that when a stranger comes to your door, he must share your table.

Papa answered the door, and there were two big men who asked if he was Morris Burns. Papa nodded his head. They asked, Do you have some schnapps? Papa invited them to sit at the table with Mamma and me.

We were just beginning the end of the Sabbath. Papa broke the bread, dipped it in salt for the spice of life, and handed a piece to all at the table.

Then Papa filled the glasses with schnapps and said the blessing, and the glasses were raised to the lips and the contents put down in one swallow.

The two men coughed, stood up, flashed a badge, and each took Papa by a hand and put on handcuffs. And there they went through the door, with Papa saying to Mamma, It's a pogrom, like in Russia —hide the child...here in the golden land, America? A pogrom?

Mamma could only scream, Morris, take your coat, it's winter outside! but they were gone before he could take it from her outstretched hands. The front door slammed shut and Mamma and I spent the rest of the night terrified, and crying into Papa's coat.

It was Saturday night and we didn't know where to go. A neighbor told us to go to the Relief Society, but they could not get a bond that late on Saturday night. Papa spent the night in jail.

On Sunday, Papa was released, and when Mamma and I got there, Papa—who always said he was unafraid of anything, that he was Samson—stood there facing Mamma who took one look at him and said, Some Samson—you're yellow. Then we went home.

Monday morning we were all in court, in the first row. They called Papa's name. Papa spoke two words in English: Morris and Burns. Some man stepped up to Papa and held out a black book and put Papa's left hand on it. He pushed Papa's right hand up and said, Repeat after me... All the time the man was pushing Papa around and speaking, Papa kept turning to me in the first row and asking what the man was mumbling. I tried to translate, but before I could say The man says... Papa was on the chair.

Mamma, always a great help in an emergency, was speaking Gaelic Irish with a policeman—New York's finest. She was up to, And begorra you're not just saying that... when the judge started to read something out loud, something that went on and on and ended with Guilty or not guilty. Papa kept looking to me to translate; Mamma was going full speed ahead in her conquest of the Irish, and the judge was shouting, Guilty or not guilty?

Papa kept saying, What does he mean—gilly, golly, gooly?

That was it. The judge brought down the hammer and the words, Guilty. Pay fifty dollars. In golden America, the pogrom was over

Well, Papa still made the schnapps, but he kept it for family use only, and whenever there would be a knock on the door Saturday nights, Mamma would say, Morris, your friends are back. Quick— get the good schnapps. '

Long of Hair and Short of Sense

In our household the old laws governed. Papa was the king in business. Mamma the queen of the home. These two laws made Mamma's and my life exciting and third law made it wonderful. As Papa explained it: A man must never make his wife weep, for God counts her every tear.

Mamma bought a Persian lamb fur coat then found out a few weeks later that the in thing was Hudson seal. So, Mamma bought a Hudson seal, and when Papa came home she dolled up and strutted into the sitting room saying, Nu, how do I look? To Papa,

Mamma always looked like the best thing God ever created in his six days of hard work. When Mamma would point at a woman walking down the street who had three chins, a fifty-four inch bust, and was tall, as an example of beauty (Mamma always tried to keep her chin down to try to make double chins), Papa would always say, Rose, your behind is nicer than all of her. Mamma would say he did not appreciate true beauty, and the conversation stopped there.

So, now she was modeling the Hudson seal, and Papa of course said, To me you always look gorgeous—even naked. Then, suddenly, Papa said: But Rose, what happened to the little curls in the fur? Did they come out in the rain? Persian lamb is curly and Hudson seal is straight, just like human hair.

No, Mamma replied, this is not the Persian lamb. It is the latest thing: Hudson seal. Isn't it gorgeous?

Papa began to say, But Rose, you just got the Persian.... but never finished the sentence because Mamma was already pulling the long hair pins out of her bun to let her hair down. The theory Mamma worked on is if woman is long of hair and short of sense, what do you expect? Wisdom?

Papa got the idea and told Mamma the coat looked beautiful. He knew he would have to bathe and get dressed to go out. You just don't get the latest fashion and stay home, as Mamma would say, for the mice to admire you.

Experts

In Russia, Papa had been a Talmudic student, which was considered the highest calling. This meant that his life would be devoted to studying scripture, and his wife's family would be devoted to supporting his family for the honor.

In America, Papa wrote plays for the Jewish theater, and when he met Mamma, she thought he was a brilliant writer. After they were married, Mamma said writing was woman's work and that Papa should go into business. The proper description would be to go into and out of businesses, which they did with regularity. By this time, I had come along and was about five years old when a friend of Papa's offered to sell him a rag business. Papa went to work for him to learn what it was all about. In those days they used to sort rags by cottons, woolens, silk, etc., for recycling.

After a couple of days on the job, Papa came home shouting, We don't need to buy a rag business, Rose, we are rich! With that, Papa said: Look, I found this and the stupid man said I could have it, showing Mamma a handkerchief that was soiled and tied on the four corners. Look, Rose, we're millionaires—diamonds—'ta whole handkerchief full!

Mamma said nothing, but pulled up a kitchen chair to the telephone, and immediately called her sister Helen in Asbury Park, New Jersey. Helen was the family expert on diamonds.

Mamma hung up the phone after listening carefully. Then, taking the handkerchief from Papa, she took me by the hand and walked me into the back guestroom, shutting the door. Not a single word was exchanged between Papa and Mamma.

Like I said, Mamma stood 4 feet 11 inches and was a Humpty Dumpty on chicken legs. First she drew the black window shades, and then the white. Then she pushed the bed into the wall. She got down on her stomach and wiggled all the way to the far corner.

Then she said, Pull me out, and I did

Mamma threw open the door and said: Schmuck! Diamonds? They're glass! They don't sparkle in the dark! If you know as much about rags as you do about diamonds, don't buy the business. Let's eat. And it was all over after Mamma tied the handkerchief back and threw it at Papa.

A couple of days later, Papa came home excited again. Rose, I met a man and he said he would trade me land in Atlantic City for the glass, so I agreed, and here is our deed. We're rich!

Are there any buildings on the property? Mamma asked.

No, Rose, replied Papa, only sand—it is about a square block near the main street and the boardwalk.

What's only sand and ocean? Can you rent out the boardwalk? Schmuck. With that, Mamma twisted the deed into a long stick, gave Papa a zetz (whack) on the head, and wanted to know if his friend's sand equaled the glass pebbles. We ate supper, and never mentioned it.

About a week later, Papa came home, and this time he knew that the expert would know what he had. Rose, said Papa, I met some schmuck who gave me forty dollars for the Atlantic City deed.

Now, said Mamma, that's rich. Let's eat and go to the theater, and with what we'll have left over, I can buy the child a new outfit.

Now Atlantic City will be gambling. Big deal. Over fifty years ago, Papa gambled on Atlantic City too and won forty dollars.

Don't Tell Mama — It Is Our Secret

I don't think Papa was unhappy to have an only child—and a daughter at that. There was no son to carry on the name, but adjustment was no problem. God gave Papa a girl and who argues with God? Papa told Mamma when I was born: Rose, we don't have a child, we have an angel.

Being an angel only meant I was not responsible for religious matters. I became Papa's sidekick in the cellar, learning how to splice wires, saw wood and tin, repair plumbing, drive a nail straight, and how to straighten a bent nail.

The cellar was a cold, damp place, but Papa always sang and told stories, and I loved to be with him, and loved working together. It didn't matter that the toy box looked like a coffin—we stood it up, put shelves in it, and it became a storage box before Mamma could find out and kid us.

One bitter, cold night, I noted blood all over everything. Pa, where is all this blood coming from? I said.

Shh, Papa cautioned me, don't let Mamma hear the word blood —you know what'll happen.

Drug stores used to close at ten o'clock in the evening and it was almost that now. I had to tell Mamma that Papa had scratched himself and we needed peroxide and bandages. Mamma bundled me into wool sweaters, coat, boots, etc., and we hurried over the snow to the drug store. Mamma was too excited about our dog getting ready to have puppies to give much thought to the first aid supplies.

Mamma always bought the biggest, or by the dozen or the gross to save money and have plenty on hand. We got the biggest bottle of peroxide, the largest roll of bandage, and the largest spool of adhesive tape. Band Aids had not yet been invented.

I got back to Papa with the purchases, and Mamma went back to put together the apple crate box for the coming puppies. I went to help Papa but, as usual, Papa said that in Russia they knew everything, and he could do it himself. Humming and singing, and since a little is good, a lot is better, Papa went to work. First, he poured the whole bottle of peroxide on his arm; then he used the entire roll of bandage; finally, all the adhesive. See, he said, I can do it myself. He had bandaged his arm from the wrist to the elbow. We went back to work sawing wood.

Pa, I screamed, where is all the blood coming from?

Shh, he said, Mamma will hear you.

He had bandaged the wrong arm. He kept the bandage on for a week, so Mamma wouldn't find out and laugh, and then sarcastically tease him his own words, in Russia we know it all.

Who Was Scared? I Was Just Worried

After WWII, I took a very lucrative sales position with a Canadian paper company, which included the use of a chauffeur and limousine. I gave my chauffeur the weekend off except for the rare occasions when I had to do business. One weekend, there was no business to be done and Mamma decided we should go out by ourselves and that I would drive the limousine. Not fond of driving, I wanted to relax that day, but who could argue with Mamma? Especially since she wanted to go to Canada.

Although the Canadian border was still patrolled, we had gone back and forth all the time, so I didn't give it a thought. We got in just fine.

Shopping is always part of a trip, so we bought my daughter Toby some toys, and the saleslady said to put them in the trunk and not bother to declare them as the amount was minimal. That sounded reasonable, and it would save time going back across the border into America.

The US border guard asked whether we had anything to declare, and I simply answered, No. Then, unexpectedly, he went to the rear window and asked Mamma: Where were you born? That did it.

Mamma had resided in the United States for forty-seven years. She had taken out her First Paper twice, but never got her final papers because she could not understand how George Washington could be the First Father of his country when Lincoln freed the slaves. Consequently, Mamma was declared an alien during the war, and now with a uniformed official addressing her, she froze.

The official came back to my window, asked me to step out of the car and open my trunk. Now I froze.

The trunk cleared inspection, but he again went back to his interrogation of Mamma, who by this time looked like she had been frozen in an upright, wide eyed condition.

Where were you born? he asked again, and then again.

Finally, Mamma turned to me and started speaking Yiddish hysterically, saying they were going to imprison her as a spy. The officer, hearing Mamma speak at last, asked: Where did you last vote?

Now Mamma knew she was a pigeon, and she turned another stone face to the official. Suddenly, as though a stroke of genius hit, the official said: She's deaf, and with that he stuck his head in the window and shouted his question into Mamma's face. Now Mamma really started pouring out the Yiddish to me. She told me about her coming to this country at thirteen years of age, and how she had tried to get her citizenship, and how she was not an alien, and should not be arrested and deported, etc. etc.

Now here come the really odd part; I was hearing Yiddish and the official was hearing an entirely different language.

The official stepped from my Mamma's side of the car and came around to my side. Lady, I have never heard such beautiful Gaelic spoken—I wish you would ask your mother to say something more."

I knew that to do this, all I had to tell Mamma was, There's nothing wrong, everything is okay now, and Mamma would attack. And she did, starting with, Okay, schmokay. The officer stood there with his both ears cocked like the dog on the old Victor Victrolas, his eyes far away in the Scottish Highlands where Gaelic was spoken. Meanwhile, I'm watching all this and wondering if I'm still on the same planet with these same two people.

Finally Mamma broke into tears, and the official apologized for detaining us, and waved us on. When we were out of sight of the station, I pulled over to the side of the road because Mamma's tears had turned to torrential tears of laughter, and we exhausted ourselves laughing.

I don't know what happened to me, Mamma said, but when I heard him ask you to open the trunk I knew we were going to jail, and then when he questioned me, I really got scared because going to jail with you and Toby would mean that we at least were together. Being an alien meant we would be separated. And what is Gaelic, anyhow?

I didn't know then, and I suppose I'll never know. I can only imagine that Gaelic is one of those magical mysteries in life that only works when you do not understand it. Like a gift horse. Don't look it in the mouth.

If the House Smells Good,
Let It Be Dirty

We don't have busy hands anymore—that's why we don't have good smells in the house. All of a sudden I smelled my kitchen—pooh—it was antiseptic. I took a deep breath and recalled the smells of my childhood, and decided to bake a yeast cake. So it didn't look like Duncan Hines or Betty Crocker, but it looked like llamas: fat here, skinny there. When you put your teeth in it, you had something to chew on and to smell—oh to smell. It didn't go up like it should. I put it near the heater like the directions said for it to rise. Later I remembered that Mama put the dough in bed and tucked it in under a down pillow where it would rise big and round and smooth and delicious to smell.

At Purim, which is like Halloween, I told my boys we were going to bake and they should invite their friends to help. I cleared the kitchen table, set out the recipe and all the ingredients, and then sat by as a coach. They mixed and kneaded, let the dough rise, and mixed and kneaded again. Then I showed them how to fill small cakes and make many different shapes.

The cakes were delicious. The shapes defied description, but they were not store made, machine made. They had been hand sculptured.

The friends were all given little cakes to take home to their parents. The following day was Purim, and the kids were asked if they wanted to make the rounds with us, distributing the little cakes and getting money.

I called all my relatives and friends to advise them we were coming, and coached them about the proper thing to do. Accept the little cakes, and give the kids some change. All the adults were excited about the visits, and where there were children, we promised to let them join the fun the following year.

Our last stop was at an old folks home. They had just finished dinner, and had before them the store bought, machine-shaped dummy cakes. Then my kids appeared. The most joyous laughter filled the dining room, and the cakes were being gobbled up in spite of the nurses running about screaming, You can't eat that! They did, and all the happy memories of their own childhood mingled with their tears of joy. What a haul for the kids—they were loaded with coins and paper money, but their happiness and self satisfaction could not be described.

Last week I baked bagels with my grandchildren and their little friends. The bagels had no holes, or were straight sticks, small, large, fat and skinny—but oh what joy to eat hot bagels with butter —bagels you made yourself.

Try it.

Businessmen Don't Make
Good Friends Sometimes

Papa decided he wanted to be a farmer. Why? Because a good friend of a good friend knew of a good farm. They said it had five thousand chickens, twelve cows, and in the summer season would accommodate one hundred guests. Papa was all for buying it, on paper, but Mamma insisted on investigating it. The trip proved that there were five hundred chickens, one cow, and if summer guests liked sleeping in the open air, it could accommodate one thousand.

Then Papa heard of a candy store for sale. This time Mom and I investigated. We stood across the street half the day and night to watch the trade, and it looked like a real winner. We bought it.

The cigar boxes were empty, the candy boxes were empty, the ice cream cans were empty except for some on top of padded paper.

That was the first surprise.

The second surprise was no trade. Where did all the customers go to? A drunk finally told us. The people had used the store for a bootlegging front and had taken their operation elsewhere.

We owned the empty store and the house, and no one checked about insurance. In a few weeks it burned to the ground.

Florida Water Is Bitter

Mamma got wind that it had become fashionable to go to Florida in the summer as well as winter. Since I could not dissuade her, I agreed, but for one week only. Mamma agreed and we were on our way.

When we stepped from the air-conditioned train onto the Miami platform, we thought something struck us all sick—we couldn't breathe, and choked so we could hardly speak. The porter explained that it was the heat and high humidity, so Mamma immediately pooh poohed it and adjusted.

We always spent the first day shopping, because the styles were different, and it also serves the purpose of acquainting you with the new city.

On the second day, Toby, who was four years old then, woke up with a sore throat. The doctor prescribed medication, and also fresh orange juice. Not having a container to get the juice, I emptied a large bottle of shampoo into two water glasses, washed the bottle and went to get the juice.

When I returned, Mamma was sitting on Toby's bed drinking the shampoo. She said, Florida water is bitter. It's not water, Mamma, I shouted, it's shampoo!

No wonder it's bitter, Mamma said and started to scream I'M POISONED! Each time she said poisoned, bubbles poured out of her mouth. She was a very active bubble machine, and everything Toby and I did to comfort her only made Mamma scream poison more.

Then Mamma began contagious laugh, and the more we all laughed, the more she bubbled. When Mamma decided that she was all laughed out, she went to the bathroom and stuck her finger down throat.

Moments later, she returned wiping the edges of her mouth with a hand cloth and said, Well, what are you waiting for? It's time to go on the sightseeing tour.

Damn the heat. Damn the humidity. Damn the bubbles. Mamma was on vacation and that was that.

Run with the Horse

In Brooklyn on Ocean Parkway, they had two islands: one had a bicycle path and benches, and the other had a bridle path. I preferred to stay inside the rink and let the horse dance to the music. Mamma used to think I was a regular genius with the horses, but actually, other than getting all dressed up in black riding habit with a derby, my job ended as soon as I mounted up. When the music started, the horses danced, and we smiled and sat the saddle. Occasionally, I would take the horse through Prospect Park, but since the time my horse decided to be two-legged on the trolley tracks with traffic going like crazy around the Arch, I didn't trust horses much.

Then, one cool evening as I was cantering along the path feeling perfectly safe when a mounted patrol officer galloped by me. My horse did not follow the lead but I had to rein my horse to a two legged stop. A car had hit the officer's horse, and just when I got there, the officer was putting a bullet in its head.

Oi—I did not leave the academy for a long time. But when spring was in the air and the evenings grew long, I ventured out again. I was walking my horse and humming to myself when I heard Mamma scream, "That's her—that's my daughter! Across from me on the other island was Mamma and her friends also taking in the spring air.

That was the only time I used my riding crop—to salute friends along the way.

What are you doing? Mamma screamed across four lanes of traffic.

Riding, I replied.

Run with the horse! Mamma screamed back.

But Mamma, I called back, last night a policeman had to kill his horse at this intersection because an automobile hit it.

Kill, schmill—run with the horse, you coward, you! '

Well, I ran with the horse—until I got to the next intersection out of sight of Mamma and her friends, at which point I turned the horse from the bridle path to the sidewalks of New York. I can still hear the clatter of horseshoes on the sidewalks and gutters. All the way, I gently talked to the horse, apologizing for taking him off the soft bridle trail.

When I got home, the coward was a heroine. Mamma said I rode just like the Austrian cavalry—shtultz (proud and erect). I was still proud and still erect, because I had not let Mamma down, and still did not run my horse to death.

A Piano Doesn't Mean Piano Lessons

When Mamma bought me a piano, it caused quite a stir in New York, and especially because we lived on the fourth floor. This meant that the piano movers hoisted the piano up on ropes past all the fire escapes and windows, finally swinging it into the house through the window opening.

Immediately, I sat down and with one finger picked out My country 'tis of thee, sweet land of liberty, of thee I sing. Mamma heard it and came running and screaming, Play it again! I did.

With that, Mamma picked up the telephone and called the music teacher to cancel the first lesson, saying: Listen, they just delivered the piano. My daughter, the genius, is already playing so good, she can teach you.

That was the beginning and the end of piano playing for the genius. We dragged that piano around with us from apartment to apartment, because in New York you only lived nine months in the apartment and three months at the shore or in the mountains.

After paying for schlepping the piano around—which cost fourty dollars each time, we left it in a fifth floor apartment, figuring we'd let the landlord worry about it.

I can still play My Country 'Tis of Thee with one finger—such a genius.

Books Have Other Purposes

To get promoted you had to bring in a notice from the doctor that your tonsils had been removed; a note from the dentist that you had no cavities; and a ticket from the penny weight scale to show how much you weighed.

My tonsils and teeth were no problem, but bringing in a penny scale ticket that said I was 149 pounds at ten years of age was too much.

I waited for my best friend Ettie to get out of school, and then put her on the scale. She weighed 80 pounds. I couldn't get away with that.

So, starting with 80 pounds, we stopped kid after kid, and added textbooks to Ettie, until after twelve cents, we came up with a ticket I thought could pass. It read: 120.

That accomplished, we set out for the candy store to get a chocolate malt because we were so exhausted trying to put weight on.

If You Want to Teach,
Reach the Student

In my senior year in high school, the dean called me in and asked me to tutor a fourteen year-old freshman girl in French. The parents were rich, it was 1934, and the dean made it a personal request. Hesitant to accept this assignment, I nonetheless reported to the girl's home as requested.

The family left the house so we could have quiet. I sat in the dining room for forty-five minutes and was about to leave when down the stairs came a teenage Lady Godiva, wrapped in only a bath towel, with her beautiful blonde hair flowing as she walked.

I knew I shouldn't have come, and after a brief attempt at conversation, took off happily, rid of a problem

The dean got after me again. Boy, rich parents are very convincing, and they convinced the dean that Lady Godiva wanted to learn French. Baloney, but I was on the hook.

After the third week of collecting dough for watching Blondie prance around, I finally offered her a deal.

If I teach you how to get every guy at a party, will you agree to learn French? She lit up with delight, and I taught her my part of the bargain first.

Here's how it works: when you go to a party, and the statistics are six girls to every boy, you fix your hair with bangs, in the French style. Then you speak with zee French aksant, like zees, an you say your ship she jus arrive from Paris—and how much you luv zees kontry.

She settled down to French lessons and had no trouble catching guys.

Two years later I received a phone call to say that she had become the editor of the French paper in school, and a member of La Société Française.

The French have a phrase for it: OO LA LA.

Stealing Can Mean Healing

I have always considered myself blessed in my friends, from childhood through adulthood. Being an only child, every one of my friends became a sister or a brother to me. I never looked for faults, and so found none. Virtue of a friend was in loyalty and being together every possible moment.

My dearest friend, I'll call her Mary, thought it was her calling in life to satisfy my every wish or want, and so she was always bringing me little presents like a kite, a top, jacks, etc. I accepted with delight, and never even thought to question where she was getting the stuff from.

The whole neighborhood buzzed with excitement when a new Woolworth opened, with a million items we had not seen before and with so many items costing only a nickel or a dime. It was great just walking through the store and fingering the beads, the dolls, the toys, and hoping you could just have it all.

Mary and I were going through the store one day and I fell in love with a ceramic bird which cost $1.29. Oh how much I wanted to give Mamma that bird for Mother's Day, but I didn't have the money. I mentioned it to Mary when we were a block away from the store, and she whipped the bird out from under her sweater and handed it to me. I was thrilled and excited, but then realized how Woolworth had been fulfilling my dreams through Mary. I got scared and told her never to do it again, and especially never to do anything like that when she was with me. That being over, we ran home to wrap the bird and surprise Mamma with it on Mother's Day.

Several weeks later, Mary and I were going up and down the aisles again at Woolworth's, and I stopped to admire some beads, so tiny you could hardly string them, and they had about ten strings of them to make up a necklace. Mary and I were standing side by side when we were grabbed by the neck of our sweaters and spun around. There stood the manager, and he was shouting something at us about stealing the beads.

I was scared, but more than that I was angry. I had not taken any beads.

Then he said, Empty your pockets, and he looked right at me. Well, we had just been playing hopscotch, or potsy as we called it, and my favorite things to throw into the boxes were banana peels and pieces of broken glass, which were in my pockets. I also had three or four handkerchiefs, man size, because I had a cold. I started pulling out handkerchiefs, jacks, balls, banana peels, until the manager got impatient. He stuck his hand in my pocket and cut his fingers on my broken pieces of glass. Mary had no pockets. And now with a bleeding finger, he told us to get out of the store and never come back.

I was hurt, angry, and the tears were beginning to fall as we started toward the door. When we got past one counter away from the manager, Mary said, Run. I said, Why? I'm no crook. Now she screamed, Run! and I finally did, and as I did I heard beads hitting the hard terrazzo floor. The harder I ran, the more the beads kept spilling from my pocket. The sound of those beads hitting the floor, and then jumping around in the air finally scared me, and we were several blocks away from Woolworth's when I asked Mary what happened.

Well, she had slipped the beads into my pocket because her sweater had no pockets, and when the manager squeezed his hand in he not only cut his finger, but cut the strands of beads.

When she saw how scared I was, she promised never to ever again steal anything when she was with me. I made a promise to myself to never, ever again say I liked something in front of Mary.

Fire, Police, Ambulance

I had two best friends: Katie, whose mother was addicted to gambling, and Ettie, whose mother made and sold bootleg booze. What we all had in common was the fact that all the mothers were otherwise engaged (mine was in business) and we were free agents.

To parents, I was always the brilliant A student, good kid Laurie in whom all trust reposed. They never figured me to be the draykup —the leader who always got crazy ideas, and in order to have Ettie and Katie go along, had to make them lie to their parents. We were all fifth graders, and were not supposed to travel the subway by ourselves. I wanted to go to the Brooklyn Museum, and I never had any problem getting money. I just punched the cash register and Papa or Mamma would kiss me on the head and say Good girl. Ettie and Katie had to lie to get money; they said we were going to the neighborhood movie. We packed lunches in Katie's house, and took off.

The museum was breathtaking, and the mummies truly scared us, but not so much that we'd lost our appetite. As our frightened breathing slowed, I noticed that it was lunch time and suggested we have lunch in an old stagecoach which was on display.

All we have to do is to pull down the shades so they can't see us, I assured my friends. With that, each of us pulled on a different shade at precisely the same moment, which started a chain reaction. To our horror, the whole coach began to fall apart, making the most awful sounds. Run! ' I screamed, and the metal taps on my shoes hitting against the marble floor made it easy to track us, so I kicked them off and we got out.

Now, what to do. It was only lunch hour and we couldn't go back into the museum—beside which, I didn't have any shoes. So, I said we ought to go to Prospect Park, which was right there, and fish for tadpoles. That way we could take them home, let them grow into frogs, and then take them to the subway at night when the girls got home from work and scare them. We could hide frogs easier than mice, which we used to use, but had to quit because the string would not stay on their tails.

We waded, and fished, and all I got was a big cut on my foot because I was barefoot. Then we were chased out of the park too, because wading was not permitted.

Well, we thought we might as well go home. I thought we should ride in the front train, because then we could stand near the engineer and see where we were going. That was exciting, and we could see the train whiz into the stations, and back out into darkness. What we couldn't see was that the train was headed not to Brooklyn, but in the opposite direction: the Bronx. We were late —oh were we late, and I couldn't think of anything except what was waiting for us at home.

Ettie and Katie wouldn't have too much trouble. They didn't mind getting spanked. I never got spanked—I got looked at. That hurt more than a dozen spankings.

Sure enough, there was the ambulance, the fire engine and the police cars, and I knew Mamma was worried. So I went back around the corner, climbed to the roof of several buildings away from us—jumped from roof to roof until I got to my house. Then I went down a straight ladder to the third floor, down the fire escapes to the first floor, and with a rusty old nail file I kept just for that purpose, opened the window lock and stepped into my bedroom.

I combed my hair, put on shoes, and marched out of my room asking, What's the matter, Mamma? I got screamed at, beamed at, hugged and kissed. The firemen, policemen, and ambulance people were all thanked by Mamma for being so nice to come.

I didn't get looked at because when I showed Mamma the cut on my foot that I had gotten on a broken bottle in the movies, Mamma got so mad at the slobs who do not clean the theaters, that I was saved. Greater relief came when I learned that Mamma could not go down and beat the theater people up because she had an important business meeting the next day.

Two Pocketbooks and the
Third Was God's

The house was so big, we shut off the front rooms in the wintertime so we would not have to heat them. If company came, we would just light a fire in the fireplace a couple of hours before they arrived, and the living room would be just right.

I never had to ask Mamma if I could have friends over. I had been instructed early in life that the house was mine as much as theirs. It went without saying, though, that you had to have respect for things, as well as people. My friends were well-behaved, and I never had any problem. As a matter of fact, they always helped me clean house so we could all have more time to play

The game was hide and go seek, and I went into the cold closed living room and stood up in the fireplace chimney. Something fell down, and I picked up a leather coin purse with two pockets, jammed with paper money to bursting. I was just thrilled and could hardly wait for Mamma to come home so I could get my reward and treat all my friends to Chinese food, movies, ice cream, frankfurters, and cream soda pop. Wow!

Mamma and Papa came home together that night, and when I excitedly handed Mamma the purse, we both noticed Papa's face, and we knew. But Mamma said, See, our child is an angel of God, and his messenger, I was just praying for a little something from Heaven so we could go to the theater tonight—they are opening the special play.

Papa said nothing. We ate dinner and headed out, dressed to the hilt, for the theater. Just before we got there, Mamma handed Papa the change purse saying, Here—it was your prayers to God that really brought it, so you spend it.

Papa just took the purse and said nothing, because he knew what Mamma was thinking. She always said that the only partnership you could trust was between a husband and a wife, and that in a marriage, there cannot be two pocketbooks. Papa wanted to buy something special for himself, and since he was not

44

long of hair and short of sense, and it appeared a foolish thing, he tried to hide it from Mamma.

They went together to buy it: a beautiful embroidered satin bag in which to keep his prayer shawl, the Talith. Mamma's only comment was: Morris, it is not foolish, it is beautiful—as beautiful as you.

Don't Worry — I'll Hold Your Hand

Two things had been absolutely forbidden me: a bicycle and skates. Papa, with reason, believed they were dangerous on the streets of New York, especially when you crossed streets.

Mamma, on the other hand, made sure I got the first thing that came out and had the best. When I was twelve, she got me Russian boots with high heels. I loved my sneakers, but for Mamma, I wore the heels.

One day she put five dollars in my palm and said, Go buy skates —all the other kids are skating and you're not. I was a coward, really, and didn't want skates. But Mamma said skates, so I went.

I hid the skates under the bathtub, which stood on legs, so Papa wouldn't see them. Mamma came home early and immediately asked to see them. I crawled under and produced the skates, and Mamma shrieked, What kind of skates are these? The crooks! I told her they were learner's skates and had wooden wheels so you wouldn't go too fast. Well, we went fast, with the skates, right back to the hardware store and exchanged them for a pair of ball bearing Unions, and Mamma had to see how they worked immediately.

We were on a steep hill street when Mamma had me put the skates on. Then, taking my hand, she helped me to the middle of the sidewalk facing the downhill street, saying, Don't worry, I'll hold your hand.

She held my hand on the level part then, facing the slide, she gave me a good push, and I was on my way downhill lickety-split. There was a telephone pole at the bottom of the street and I just headed for that, wrapped around it and stopped.

Mamma ran downhill after me screaming what a genius her daughter was —in a minute I was already skating.

Actually, I was cured of any desire to skate, so I took them apart and built a skate wagon using a base board and an apple crate. I nailed two pieces of wood in a V-shape to form the handles. I propelled myself by riding with one foot and pushing with the other. Now Papa said, Such a genius—a real mechanic—better than a boy, believe me. It didn't bother Mamma at all since she already knew I could skate like a champion and professional.

Doctors, Butchers, and Dishes

The pain started on the Sabbath—Friday night—and it was intense. Papa diagnosed the trouble right away: Indigestion. I ate Bolls Rolls, a fix laxative, Ex-Lax and washed it down with a lemon flavored fizz laxative called Magnesia.

Saturday morning came and I was still rolling on the floor with pain. Now Papa had to rely on his old Russian remedy, which was so fascinating to watch that I would have moments of wonderment when the pain would disappear.

Papa put a great big pot on the stove and brought the water to a boil. Then he took a Turkish towel and carefully rolled it up the long way. Twisting it, he held the ends while he dipped the middle into the hot boiling water and then rang it out. These hot compresses were applied to my stomach. Nothing worked. Mamma did not like doctors, and on Saturday, doctors took the day off anyway. By Saturday night, it was ambulance time. Mamma asked the driver to go fast and make the siren loud—she thought it was one of the greatest rides she had ever been on. You have to laugh, pain or no pain, when Mamma laughed. She was an expert at enjoying things.

At the hospital, all was quiet. St. Catherine's was a Catholic hospital and everyone was getting ready for a special midnight mass. I was dressed in the hospital open back gown and was helped into a high bed. I was so busy watching the nurses and Mamma that I had no pain at all, and figured Papa's remedy had worked. There were a lot of old people in the ward where I was put, and they all got up to welcome me. I was the center of attraction and was not aware that Mamma, who had been making friends also, had left, until she came bursting in.

Did you swallow any orange pits? she asked. I said I had not. Did you eat any frankfurters? I said I had not.

Then came the order from Mamma the expert

Get out of bed—get dressed—we are going home. They want to operate, those butchers. If you didn't swallow orange pits or eat frankfurters, you don't have an appendix. Move.

Then, folding her hands across her chest, she drew herself up to her full 4 feet 11 inches and planted her feet, standing guard while I got up. I felt so sorry to leave all the nice friends I had already made who were all watching silently.

The head nurse came in, and going to the other side of the bed from Mamma, said, Child, it is almost midnight. If we do not operate, your appendix will burst and you will die. The choice is yours.

Some choice. If they didn't operate I'd die; if they did, Mamma would kill me. I thought if it was a certainty that I would die without an operation, then at least with an operation I had a chance. So I explained this to Mamma. She responded, Alright, if you believe them instead of me, go—get your operation. But remember, if you die, it's your own fault, and with that she stormed out to sign the consent form.

The last thing I remembered was hearing the bells tolling midnight, and seeing black stars on white background and vice versa after they put the ether cap on me.

I woke the next day to all kinds of goodies. All the people in the ward had given me their flowers and candy. I was the happiest kid in the world.

Then here came Mamma. She never walked. She always filled the room even before she entered it with her quick steps, and it was always as though beautiful electric rainbow sparks danced around her. Before I could say hello, Mamma sized up the situation and said, Well, I can see they didn't operate after all. See—I told you. Alright, get dressed and come home. When I told Mamma I had had the operation, she could not believe it because, as she said, You look like a doll.

I had to show her before she would believe me, and now that it was all over, and I looked like a doll, Mamma ran out to get everybody, including nurses, ice cream, candy, and flowers.

In those years, you were hospitalized for fourteen days after surgery. Mamma had time to make friends with everyone and anyone connected with St. Catherine's. You were not allowed to get out of bed, so when the time came to be discharged, I was taken from the bed to the wheelchair, and for the moment that I put my feet on the floor, they just collapsed under me.

Mamma had the cab ready, and where did the cab stop? At home for just so long as it took for Mamma to throw all the stuff I brought home into the house. Then she just jumped back into the cab and away we went to the movies.

But Mamma, I said, the doctor and nurses said I should go straight home to bed.

Bed, schmed, Mamma sang back, it's a good picture, a double feature with vaudeville yet, and you'll forget to be sick watching it. After all, it is already two weeks since the operation and besides, I can't miss the dishes they are giving away this week—it will break up my set '

Mamma was right. The movie made us laugh so much I forgot to be sick.

Years later, when Toby needed to have an infected tooth pulled under sedation I got her excited by saying, You better hurry up or we will miss the new Walt Disney movie. She ran into the dentist's office and jumped on the chair. Her first words when she awoke, without tooth, were, Are we late? And we both ran out of the dentist's office past the nurses and doctor who stood there with blank expressions and you could read their minds: She must be crazy.

I was just like Mamma. Toby did not even remember having the tooth pulled while she ate her ice cream cone and frankfurter and watched the Walt Disney movie. We had made it just on time.

If You Are Going to Drink
— At Least Enjoy It

The war was over: Japan had surrendered. We were in Far Rockaway that summer, at the beach. I organized a block party, and all the people on the block contributed $1.00 per adult and 50¢ per child to their own house fund. Each house had an average of thirty tenants, not including children. Our house decided to buy beer and whisky. I got the police to cordon off our street, and then had a grandstand built and rented loudspeaker equipment. I was the Master of Ceremonies leading the parade, tap dancing, singing, etc. I was sort of tired when we got back to our house and the front porch filled with rocking chairs. Everyone was feeling great, telling jokes, and laughing. A man came by with a quart bottle, which was brown, and when it got to Mamma, he started to pour some in her glass and then stopped. Fill it up, ' said Mamma. But, said the man, when Mamma came back with:

Listen, I paid 50¢ for my granddaughter, and she doesn't drink. I paid $1.00 for my daughter and she doesn't drink—so fill it up.

The man started to say but again, but when Mamma gave him the look, he filled her tall glass.

Mamma never worried about drinking, because it seemed she had the constitution that absolutely ignored any alcoholic effects. She could drink any man under the table, and never failed to do so at weddings, Bar Mitzvahs, and other occasions.

Mamma drank the whole glass and said, Well, this is the best beer I ever drank   oi   this is REAL beer   oi   Laurie, I don't feel so good—help me into the room.

What Mamma mistook for beer was whisky, because both the beer and whisky were in brown quart size bottle. Of the sixteen ounces of liquid she had swallowed, fourteen were bourbon whisky – not beer.

Mamma turned green—really green, and began upchucking everything. I've been there and I know how terrible it can be, but to my astonishment, Mamma laughed, and laughed, and laughed, and kept saying in wonderment, I am drunk—I am finally drunk....

She would not let me call a doctor and for three days she enjoyed the fact that, at last, she had gotten her money's worth. She had always been so upset that whisky cost a lot of money (as opposed to beer) and that it never did anything to her. Now she had a cause for celebration and screamed with laughter every time she threw up. Mamma was finally getting her money's worth.

So You Can't Remember Dates?

I don't know why I always remember dates incorrectly. I always was—and even today, I still am.

New York state required graduating seniors to take State Board of Regents exams. Because I had been in advanced English classes, I had to bone up on my own.

I thought the test was set for ten-thirty Thursday morning.

Wednesday night I read Macbeth. All night, English regents papers dripped blood in my dreams.

I got up early on Thursday, did another quick review, and set out for school in Manhattan. I lived in Brooklyn, and I enjoyed the trolley trip for three cents across the Williamsburg Bridge.

I met a lot of kids leaving school. When they asked me where I was going, I said, To take my English regents. They all howled and thought it was very funny.

I got into the elevator and pushed the button for the fourth floor. The elevator stopped on the second floor, and I stepped far to the back. My dean and my English teacher got on, and I could hear them talking about some dope who was a top English student, and would not graduate because she had failed to show up for the regents.

I got out on the fourth floor. It was empty. Ugh…, did I ever fell like a dope.

How would I tell Mamma that her genius would not graduate? I didn't.

I was in the graduation exercises, so I fixed it with a friend to take a program, roll it up, and put her blue ribbon on it.

The exercises were over, and in the lobby, Mamma came running with a bouquet of twelve long stemmed American Beauty roses. She pushed the roses at me, and grabbed for the diploma. I just stood there while Mamma said, No wonder when everybody else went to the stage for a diploma I did not see you even with my eyes sticking out of my head, and she grabbed the roses and thrashed them.

This time, she said, it was not the teacher who was the dope, but her genius. We cried, and we laughed, and picked up what was left of the roses and went home and had a party.

I received a scholarship to summer school and got my diploma.

I'm still bad at remembering dates, so I understand when others have the same problem.

Who Wants to Be Alone?

Mamma loved company, especially friends of my age—whatever age that happened to be. I remember when I was twelve, Mamma gave me a birthday party. The statistics were pretty poor: we had eight girls and one boy. Mamma liked to play Post Office because she was the postman. She thought I was a rotten sport because I didn't like to kiss boys. Spin the Bottle didn't interest me either—that's where the two people at each end of the bottle, when it stops spinning, have to kiss. I was strictly a lace up sneakers kid.

At fourteen, Mamma bought me high heels and lipstick. If I got sneakers, it was only as a bribe to wear the spikes. Since I was always a fashion plate at home, we had a lot of company to see what the new thing was on the market, which of course I had first.

At fifteen, boys got more interested in me, and Mamma got very interested in them because it meant company for her. One night after dinner, I was starting to do my homework when there was a knock on the door and six boys between the ages of fifteen and seventeen walked into the living room, sat down quietly, and said, Well, here we are.

I knew right away it had something to do with Mamma who was in the kitchen humming to herself. Well, she explained, since you like to dance so much and everyone says you are so good, I organized the boys and they are ready to pay fifty cents an hour each for you to teach them how to dance. Six times fifty equals three dollars. WOW. That was a half week's depression salary. But six hours? How? Easy, I taught one, then two, then while they practiced with each other, I taught three, then four, and after the first night I collected three dollars under three hours and I was rich.

Then Mamma invited my friends Sadie and Hindu. Hindu the Magician's real name was Hilda, but when she said she wanted to drive a car to Europe, Mamma gave her the name of Hindu, which stuck. I loved them both dearly, but Sadie was even chunkier than I was and very shy, and Hindu wasn't long on brainpower. But, both didn't mind playing cards with Mamma because they knew that would guarantee them dates and parties because of Mamma's influence with me. Eventually, the dancing sessions became costly because Mamma would invite everyone to come early for frankfurters and beans, and to stay late for coffee and Danish pastry. So, I danced and danced so everyone could eat and party, but Mamma was happy, as was I.

I still do not know which was worse: having a date or not having a date. If I didn't have a date, Mamma would say, What's the matter with the boys nowadays? You're beautiful and brilliant, and you have a closet of clothes that Saks should have, and you are home Saturday night? I don't know. The boys today are crazy. No, you can't go out alone. Wait, here come Sadie and Hindu—now we can play cards and have snacks.

So, to please Mamma, I got a date for Saturday. But that did not mean that I would be alone. I had plans for Hindu and Sadie. They could play cards with her.

But Mamma never liked to take without giving, so what did she give in return for the company? A date, and who got the blind date? Me of course. Provided the both had a friend for Hindu or Sadie.

The order came down from above: You either take Hindu or Sadie on a date, or you don't go. This way, there was always someone to keep Mamma company.

I had two very busy years between fifteen and seventeen because I had to keep finding new dates. The old ones invariably became angry with the blind dates I had arranged for their friends.

When I was seventeen we moved away, and Mamma lost her two card players, but she didn't lose out because she figured another way. By this time I was working. When a boy called for a date, she would accept for me and tell me he would come at eight o'clock Saturday night. At seven o'clock that night, the doorbell would ring and in walked my date. Don't rush to dress, said Mamma, we'll have a game of cards in the meantime. He was not early; Mamma told him when to come.

If the boy was a good card player, a good sport, the game was hot, and it was eight o'clock, Mamma would say to me, You are wearing that rag on a Saturday night date? Go and change immediately. In New York this meant that you changed all accessories as well, including hat, shoes, gloves, rag and bag. The bag was the worst, because you could never fit everything into it that you had planned to carry before.

Finally, we could leave. Now came the final words: You should take good care of her; she is my only daughter, and if you come home early, we'll play another game to finish off, and have coffee and a Danish."

Actually, I found that the boys who really liked me played the game; but the other kind showed displeasure, and I soon learned to tell the boys with whom I could feel comfortable, and those with whom I always had to have my carfare home ready at all times.

Caution: Man Cleaning House

The laws, which Papa always studied and explained to Mamma and me, required that at every holiday we have something new: a whole new outfit, if you had the money. Jewish holidays come about every couple of weeks. On the big ones like the New Year and Passover, the whole new outfit was law, for it said in the books Papa studied that happy was the man who had a beautiful wife, beautiful children, and a beautiful home. This must be why Jewish men had no time to fool around or drink. And anyhow, drinking wine or schnapps was a sacramental ceremony, and a privilege not to be abused. If the man is busy carrying out the law, he is working, and since the word havoda in Hebrew means both work and prayer, work itself is holy. So again Mamma and I benefited and pranced.

It was Passover, and Mamma and I were out all day shopping. We got gorgeous outfits and stopped for the usual frankfurter and cream soda. After the refresher, Mama remembered that we had not hit one of her favorite stores, so we went shopping again.

We could hardly make it home with all the packages even though we had combined packages and stuffed things in as few boxes as we could. The problem was now: how can we tell Papa we had bought enough of 'the latest thing' to carry us through Christmas? You see, like Papa said, this was a new country which he loved, and since we were a part of it, we celebrated its customs too. Beside which, Papa told Mamma, You cannot alienate our child from her friends—if they have Christmas, so does she.

So, Mamma got a great idea. I had a bedroom and a music/study room to myself. We still had the upright piano which was carefully polished and buffed, but never played. We put the goodies we did not want in the boxes and stuck the boxes behind the piano. Now we were safe. All we had to show was what we would be wearing during the holidays.

The next day we went shopping for food, and Papa decided to clean house. That suited Mamma just fine and we trotted off to the stores. When we got home, Papa of course insisted that we inspect his work. Mamma put on her one white glove, just like she did with me when I cleaned, and started on the tour. Papa had done a tremendous job: everything sparkled and so did the piano. But, when Papa with a grand gesture moved the piano to show Mamma how thorough he was, we both froze. There were no boxes. Papa was proud of his work, but where did they go?

GARBAGE! Mamma screamed, and the two of us headed for the door. Sure enough, there they were, under coal and ashes, and yucky garbage. We found all of our boxes, crushed and garbage-soaked, but inside, the white paper was clean and our stash intact.

We carried them in the back door and put them right back behind the piano, which we knew would be a safe place—at least until the next Passover.

Who Eats Pets?

Carp fish was an integral part of gefilte fish, and gefilte fish symbolized the ideal that just as all fish live together in the ocean, so can all men live together on earth.

It was a holiday, and Mamma and I were shopping for enough food to last three days. We first stopped off at the chicken market. There, from hundreds of live chickens, Mamma found one with yellow under the wing, which you can spot after you grab the chicken and blow away the feathers.

Next we went to the fish store, and while Mamma was examining the carp and white fish, I spotted a huge live carp. Now that's a fresh carp, Mamma said, and with that she had the man weigh it and wrap it, and we carried the squirming fish home.

I drew a bathtub full of water and we put Mr. Fish in it. When Papa came home we showed him the fish and he said it looked nice and fat, but it would be better to let him in the tub a couple of days and feed him bread to fatten him up even more. Mamma was against the whole idea, but Papa knew just how to get around her by saying it would be a wonderful thing for the child.

Mamma gave in, but said, Morris, you will both get attached to the fish and then we won't have something to cook.

Pooh, said Papa. When he is big and fat I will just take the rolling pin and with one good smack on the head, it will all be over. Papa and I spent a lot of time sitting on the edge of the tub feeding the fish and watching him swim around, and Papa would tell me stories about fish from the Bible.

The day came for the fish to get clobbered, and Mamma had everything ready to go: knife, chopper, spices, and pot, and she called for Papa to come and kill the carp.

How can you kill such a beautiful and such a smart fish? Papa asked. Mamma said, I'll tell you how—here's the rolling pin.

Papa went into the bathroom with the rolling pin and came out of the bathroom with the rolling pin, but the fish was still swimming around.

Mamma started to scream about no one being able to take a bath; about the gefilte fish not getting done for the evening meal; and about how she had said in the first place that the fish would become a pet, a member of the household. Papa just hung his head, said nothing, and went into the front room.

Mamma just grabbed me by the arm, and grabbed a bunch of newspapers, and flew into the bathroom. The fish was slimy, and it took a lot of screaming, jumping, and getting wet before we finally got him wrapped up in the newspapers. He was going back to the store to get killed.

Into the shopping bag went Mr. Fish, and Mamma and I headed for the store, but the fish took a detour by wiggling and flopping its way through the newspapers and shopping bag, across the sidewalk, and into the gutter where the running water carried him swiftly to the sewer at the corner. Immediately we had an audience following us down the street as we tried to catch the fish. Some people cheered Mamma and me, but most of them cheered the fish on. Mamma finally ran ahead, sat herself right down in the water a few feet from the sewer, and caught him in her skirt. It was all over.

The fish store was right there, and when we brought him in, and the man wanted to know if we wanted the fish killed, Mamma gave him one of her Do you know what you're saying? looks and said, No, just give me another fish that's already dead. We don't eat our own pets.

The Longer the Beard, the
Bigger the Crook

Papa had a friend who lived next door with whom he went to the synagogue every day in the week and twice on Saturday. Papa had a silver beard about two inches long, and his friend had a beard down to his waistline. Mama didn't like the friend, so Papa went to pick him up to keep him from coming to our house.

Around our house we had a black wrought iron picket fence; Papa's friend's house did not. One day as I came home from school, I saw that our fence was gone. Before I could say anything to Mamma, I heard her screaming at Papa, Your friend with the long black beard—he stole our fence. I don't care if he goes with you to the synagogue every day, he's a crook! What do you mean beard and honest—with him the longer the beard, the bigger the crook, and with that Mamma grabbed me by the hand and said, Come. '

I was too scared to ask Mamma where we were going but she told me anyhow: the police station, that's where. I'll fix him, Mamma said, and your father trusts everyone—even crooks he trusts.

The police station was crowded and it seemed that we would have a long wait. But this was not for Mamma, who stood 4 feet 11 inches, had flaxen hair, blue eyes, a peaches and cream complexion, and knew the ways of New York's finest.

Mamma just pushed her way—and mine—through the crowd, and coming before the desk sergeant said in a loud voice, Me name is BOINS. What Irishman could resist that name? Mamma said she needed help to catch a crook, and we were on our way flanked by two Irish cops .

Mamma marched us all straight to the neighbor's house, and pointing to the cellar, said, See, my whole gate is in there.

They didn't need search warrants then, and the police just opened the cellar window. There, sure enough, was our fence.

Mamma put on some more of her Irish charm and wit, and the policemen knocked on the door, got the key, and then carried all of that wrought iron back into our front yard.

By the time Papa got home, dinner was already cooked, and Mamma just asked Papa if he had seen the fence in the yard. Papa said, See, Rose, you didn't have to worry, it was returned to us by God.

God, said Mamma. 'God' was two smart Irish policemen who understood that the bigger the beard, the bigger the crook. Your friend with the beard took the fence.

Let's go see Tom Mix tonight—you get free dishes on Wednesday night, and you are missing the soup bowl.

You Call It Boxing —I Call It Dancing

I don't know now, because I didn't even know then, why this neighbor came at me where I was sitting on the stairs embroidering a doily, and cracked me in the face. I never played with her kid; I had my own friends. It hurt so, I started to cry immediately and was still crying when Mamma and Papa came home and saw me. Usually, I never told Mamma anything someone did to me because she would beat them up, and I got to understand that friends can be enemies one day and friends the next. But this time I had no chance to cover up the tears, and when Mamma asked me who had hit me, I said the lady's name. I got up to follow Mamma and Papa into the house.

We were walking single file, with Mamma in the front carrying two sacks of groceries; me; and Papa carrying a crate of fruit. There was a long hall with three steps up and then another long hall to the apartment. Just as Mamma got to the steps, the neighbor's husband came bounding down the hall and cracked Mamma in the face. By now I didn't know what was happening—all I could think was that I had done nothing.

The man kept screaming things and saying something about going outside and fighting. Mamma and Papa just set the groceries down in the hall and we all followed the man outside to the street. Now a crowd was collecting. In New York, a good street fight will always draw a crowd. Papa and the man wound up in the middle with the crowd forming a ring around them. I remember feeling hurt and resentful because most of the young men were telling the man to hit the old man, meaning Papa. Papa had a beard and then the crowd began to scream, Kill Santa Claus!

The man kept hopping around, with his fists cuffed, and all the time Papa kept moving and watching him, and asking Mamma, Why is he dancing?

Mamma said, He is not dancing, he is boxing, which confused Papa even more and he responded with, What is this boxing?

Mamma explained that that was the way of fighting in America and then Papa got the idea. The man danced and ducked, and tried several times to hit Papa. All the time, Papa just watched him with his hands at his sides, and the crowd was getting wild.

Then Papa let go with a right, and the man fell on the bumpers of two cars, and was dazed. The fight being over, Papa just turned to Mamma and said, Let's eat, and we picked up the groceries and went into the house.

We had just finished eating when there came a knock at the door—the kind of knock the nightsticks used by the New York cops can make. The cop was looking for Morris Burns. Papa pointed to himself, but the policeman kept looking over Papa's shoulder for someone else. Mamma finally explained that the old, bearded man was truly Morris Burns. With that, the cop turned around and it was then that we saw the man who had started the fight, and he was jumping up and down and screaming, That's him!

The cop turned toward the man and, holding up the nightstick, said: Ya mean to tell me this old guy beat you up?

That's him! the man kept screaming.

Well, said the cop, ya better get outta here before I beat you up myself.

When Papa closed the door he just said, Well, he's not dancing now.

New Country — New
Name — New Luck

In the early 1900s, Ellis Island should have been called Irish Island since everyone in uniform was from Ireland and on the New York Civil Service payroll.

Papa and his three brothers got off the boat from Russia. As they filed through, they were asked to state their names. Berezofsky was foreign to the official, and after asking it be repeated and spelled three times, he shrugged and said, Your name now is Morris Burns. Next. Next was another brother, and when they started through the same procedure, the official said, Your name is Abe Berns. Next. Well, next came Sol Birns, and we all still give thanks to those wonderful Irishmen.

Papa said it was just like the Talmud said: a new name brings new luck, and with a new country and a new name, he was now reborn.

Having cleared the Immigration Authority, he was a ready for a street paved with gold. He bought some popcorn off a pushcart and held out his hand with some change. The man took a dime and returned a nickel. Papa was rich already. The man took a small coin, and gave him popcorn and a big coin. Papa spent a couple of hours exchanging dimes for nickels and popcorn, and already in a few hours, he was a millionaire.

Then came the flat: three rooms, two of which were windowless. The toilet was in the hall shared by seven families, all with children. For toilet paper you saved orange paper to look for the Golden America—wrappers and magazines or newspapers. There was no hot water, and the service tub in the kitchen was the bathtub. Heat was by featherbeds brought from Europe and made from goose down. Floors were bare wood, or oilcloth (congoleum). But everything, everywhere, was spotless. Whenever the gas went out, all you had to do was put a quarter in the gas meter in the toilet, and it went on again.

The Victrola and the Caruso records were the envy of all the neighbors, and the house was the gathering place for everyone each evening.

Papa was the breadwinner; Mamma was the Queen of the home. Papa liked to write plays about the people in his native home town in Russia. Mama said, Pooh—that's not a living for a grown man, and served her opinion up as dessert, after every meal. Mama talked; papa listened; we all ate. Psychiatrists had no patients, and divorce had no tears. Papa was the king at his business, Mama was the Queen in her home, and good sense and happiness prevailed.

Who Has Time for a Heart Attack?

I never knew when Mamma was having a real heart attack, or when she was using sickness as a Laurie stopper to make me do something I had indicated I did not want to do. Although the doctors had diagnosed Mamma as a hypochondriac and not a heart patient, I still had my doubts about doctors more than about Mamma. Mamma never went to the same doctor twice, explaining that once a doctor sees you, he thinks he knows everything wrong about you, and if you go back for something else, he never even bothers to examine you. For the same money, I get a complete examination every time I go to a new doctor, and he is listening to my complaint. I thought she had a point there.

It was Friday, and I had never seen such a torrential downpour in New York. Everything that was not attached to something was floating down the street. I was flying to Washington that afternoon and had not told Mamma because I didn't want any heart attacks from her. She had one anyhow, and we went to a doctor across the street from us, and only because I insisted.

She had seen him once before, and he diagnosed her with hypochondria. When we came out, Mamma looked at the sky and said, It's about ten-thirty, how come you are not worried about going to the office? She had guessed something.

Mom, I have to fly to Washington this morning, but don't worry, I'll be back in time for dinner.

Another heart attack—right there on the doctor's porch. I knew the remedy. Mom, do you want to fly to Washington with me?

Grabbing Toby by the hand, we skipped down the steps and flew across the gutter waters. As we I picked our way across the flooded street, Mamma shouted, What's the matter with you, I am almost packed and ready, and you will make us miss the plane!

Three times the plane took off, and three times it returned. Mamma loved it. She figured she was getting a lot of trips for the same money.

Finally airborne, Mamma turned to me and asked, Have they changed the route? It looks like we are flying over water.

No, Mamma, I said, it's not water, we are flying above the storm clouds, and I reached for a couple of aspirins hoping I could go to sleep and wake up in Washington.

I thought you said that they served a free lunch on this flight? Mamma's voice awakened me. I looked down the aisle. Everyone looked yellow and in prayer, and many had their heads buried in the Aloha bags the airlines are always so thoughtful in providing. In no time, a stench filled the cabin and suddenly there was a run on Aloha bags. I wanted to get on my feet anyway, so I walked back to the stewardess's area to inquire about lunch. I found her strapped in with her eyes tightly closed. At first, I thought she was dead or dying.

The plane began to rise and fall even more, and making it back to the seat made me want a parachute more than an Aloha bag.

As I returned to our seats, I found Mamma and Toby jumping up and down and screaming, Just like the loop the loop in Coney Island. Where is my lunch? All I could think of was what good did it do me to write $100,000 in flight insurance if we all go at the same time? That lousy insurance company—they get all the breaks.

So, where is my lunch? The stewardess gave up and brought trays for Mamma and Toby. Everyone got even sicker when they saw the trays going down the aisle.

Well, since no one else is eating, Mamma called down the aisle, bring us seconds, and an extra on dessert.

I had called the Statler Hotel from New York to reserve a room for us. My appointment was with the French Supply Council, and I instructed Mamma that if I did not get back in time, she and Toby could go to the hotel dining room and charge anything to our room.

I returned to the hotel a winner. The head of the French Purchasing Commission said that they had to capitulate to my demands since all the legal staff of the United States and France to whom they had access had been unable to determine how to beat me. When we were shaking hands, he cocked his head and asked if I was French, British, or Dutch? I shook my head No. I am Juisse, (Jewish) I replied politely.

Ah, he said, I should have known. It was really quite simple; no one ever bothered to run down my industry citation, properly quoted for another category.

I could hardly wait to tell Mamma the news, but both she and Toby were missing. Knowing Mamma, I knew there was no place we could really look. Whenever we had an appointment to meet at Radio City Music Hall, Mamma waited at the Roxy. When we were to meet at Macy's, Mamma waited at Gimbel's. What's the difference, they're the same aren't they?

Two hours later, a cab drew up to the hotel, and it seemed he had picked them up around the corner from the Statler, and taken them on a sightseeing tour of the city while trying to find an old hotel such as Mamma described (which was in Chicago). So, finally, he brought them back to the place where he had picked them up.

Finally, I could get back to business.

The firm had given me money to fly two ways, so I figured if we took the train back, the airfare would almost cover the train fare back for all of us.

Now it was time for me to call the boss in New York, and I asked Mamma to take Toby into the bathroom and shut the door so my boss would not know that I had taken my family along on a business trip. Mamma said Of course, and immediately left.

I had about finished making my report when Mamma opened the bathroom door, and in a nice loud voice said: Laurie, are you still talking to your boss?

She knew he would hear, and he did, and as usual, Mamma was right, He said: Burnsy, you have your mother and Toby with you don't you? How could I get out of that? Well, you did a great job. Take the weekend on us and see Washington all the way.

We certainly did. And we flew back, for as Mamma insisted, The boss said it was on him.

You Gotta Finish It

Mamma always watched the butcher, the grocer, and green man very closely to see if they were adding a finger or hand to the scales. Mamma watched pennies.

Dollars? Poch', only paper.

The Christmas we set out to get two year-old Toby a doll, I warned Mamma that I would absolutely not spend more than $5.00 on a doll that would have its head in the kitchen and body in the bathtub within an hour after we got home.

Of course, said Mamma, who could be foolish as to spend more than $5.00?

After I picked out the doll, Mamma said she would like to buy a little something else. The little something else was a Whitney doll coach marked $79.50. Toby's big real coach only cost $69.50. But, Mamma was buying, so I shut up.

Before I could pay for the doll, Mamma said, Let's give a look how it looks in the carriage. I knew it was all over for me, the doll, and my wallet. How would a $5.00 doll look in a $79.50 buggy? Like a beggar in a Rolls Royce.

Maybe you should buy this one? Mamma said of $20.00 worth of doll which she handed to Toby to put in the carriage. My shoulders dropped— I knew that from that point on it would be just a little something else.... Of course the doll fit.

Now, the poor doll would be cold without a fancy blanket and a pillow— satin, of course. And how can a doll baby in such a carriage have only one change of clothes? So now she got a nightgown and a raincoat.

Like Mamma always says, if you buy something good, it lasts, so expensive is cheap.

Years later, in California, Toby wheeled her new brother all over the neighborhood in her Whitney coach, and for 10¢ a kid could get to wheel a living, moving, crying, wetting doll around the block.

When They Invite You
to Dinner — Eat First

Other than at our own home, dinner was never served when it was supposed to be. My aunt was notorious for inviting us to dinner at six o'clock, and if lucky, we finally got to eat at eight.

We had an one hour trip to get to my aunt's house. And Mamma finally figured out how to beat her: dinner at home just before we had to leave. I was fed a full meal and Papa and Mamma had coffee and a piece of Danish pastry.

Mamma explained it this way: first of all, if the child had something in her stomach, she wouldn't get cranky; secondly, if she is not starving waiting for dinner, then when dinner is served, she will have beautiful table manners because she won't want to cram food into her mouth. So when they invite you to dinner — eat first!

If He Likes What You Make
— Love Him For It

All of our holidays were mine, for holidays were for children. According to the Scriptures, the woman of the house and the children all had to have something new for the holidays. So Mamma and I shopped for clothes, and with the same excitement, shopped for the chicken, the fish, and the groceries. Holidays were also for cleaning from the bottom up because Mamma said that guests came for a while and saw for a mile.

Mamma used to bake ruggalach. On Friday night we only had candles for light, and my friends would love to come over, sit around the dining room table, eat all the horns and drink milk, and read.

At this one holiday, Mamma, knowing how much I loved cheesecake, said that she was going to bake one for me. Papa argued in favor of apple strudel. Mamma settled the argument with: So, you bake the apple strudel, and I'll bake the cheesecake, and we'll see which is better.

Mamma baked first, because when she was done it was time for us to take baths and prepare for the Sabbath. Then Papa baked his strudel.

After dinner, when Mamma went to get the cheesecake. It was gone, and so was Papa's strudel. Papa did his best to look innocently naïve. It didn't work. Mamma and I knew he sampled the cheesecake, and had hidden it to eat it all by himself. The apple strudel he shared with us.

After Papa went to sleep, Mamma and I searched the whole house, under the beds, and even in the toilet, but never found the cheesecake. She whispered in my ear that when I got up, I was to run down to the bakery and pick up some cheese Danish for breakfast.

Then Mamma smiled. She knew that her cheesecake had been a big hit with Papa, and she was flattered. We never mentioned it to Papa, but Mamma winked at me when we served up the hot cheese Danish from the bakery.

Men Need to Louse Up

in the Kitchen Too

Sometimes Papa got a desire for certain kinds of food. One night he decided to make dumplings. Papa did everything in a big way. First, Mamma and I had to get out of the kitchen. Then he began to ask for things: Give me a ten gallon pot. So we'd come out, give him the pot and leave. Then: Where are the flour, the oil, and the stirring spoon? The kitchen soon looked like a mess, but Papa was happy, humming, humming, happy. Every once in a while he would sing out to us how lucky we were that we would get to taste dumplings just like in Russia.

When Papa asked for the baking powder, it was the first time Mamma spoke up saying that he should be careful about how much he used. Papa listened, and dumped in the whole box. Why? Because if a little is good, a lot is better, of course.

It was quiet in the house. Mamma and I were embroidering in my bedroom, when we heard wild shouts. We both ran to the door, and our shouts mingled with Papa's. There it came like hot lava, pouring through the whole house, into the bedrooms, the bathrooms, running through the hall and down the stairs. The dumplings and water were hurrying like mad to get out of the pot, and we were all jumping up and down screaming, Turn off the fire!

Every time Papa tried to get near the stove, he slipped and fell into that dumpling lava, but now that Mamma and I were there, he tried to act nonchalant. Mamma and I ran back into the bedroom so Papa wouldn't see us convulsed with laughter, because we had climbed on the bed and weren't getting burned.

We stayed in the bedroom until Papa had cleaned up the mess, and then we knew it was time to get some nice clothes on and go out to dinner and a movie.

Mamma and I said nothing, but Papa did remark that this American baking powder, it's not like in Russia—it worked too good.

The Junk Man's Dream

How much do you pay for a Singer sewing machine that is in parts? Three dollars? We'll call you right back.

Papa was fixing again, and I was making the telephone call to the junk man, as usual. He already had our grandfather clock; our Victrola with cabinet; our stove, you name it. If Mamma and I had been mechanical people we, too, would have gone to junk.

Papa had a staged routine when he became the fix it man. First, his eye would hypnotically focus on the thing to be fixed. Next, he would ask for a starched, white kitchen towel, and then when he started humming contentedly, the show was about to begin.

One by one he took the machine parts off, laying them neatly and carefully in a straight row on the white towel after having lovingly cleaned them. All the time he hummed, and he hummed, and he enjoyed.

He hummed all the way through putting all the parts back together, and when the humming grew staccato and jagged, Mamma and I knew the machine was not working anymore. (It had been working fine for us before Papa thought it needed something.)

Mamma and I knew that we still had time to call the junk man for a pickup, because Papa would always give his fix its two chances.

Now Papa's lips were pursed like a hum, but an odd grumbling whistle without tune was coming out. This time when the parts came off, they were covered with oil and Papa just threw them on the towel.

The second time around, the parts were moved into place at a heavily accelerated pace, and the whistle began to alternate with hums and humming. It was all together but would not start, and we knew we could call the junk man, because Papa would get it halfway unassembled, then with one full sweep of his arm, scatter all the pieces all over the room.

The unmistakable sound of sewing machine parts dancing on concrete basement floor told Mamma it was time to call the junk man.

His job finished, Papa came upstairs, picked up the paper, and settled down to wait for supper to be put on the table. Mamma of course had told the junk man to come after dinner had been served.

It's Not Goodbye

I told you how we lived. This is how my parents died.

PAPA

Papa was seventy-two when he died in Kings County Hospital in Brooklyn. He had called me over to his bed and said, Pray for me to die. I cannot stand all this torture they are putting me through. I have lived a good and full life and it is time for me to go. I did what Papa asked me to do, and also followed his instructions: You are not to cry for me; crying is not for the living.

Then Papa asked for Mamma and told her these two things: Rose, remarry before I am cold in my grave—do not be a burden on our only child, and, Rose, remember, when I am stretched out dead, if you walk by me naked, I'll still get up.

And in the car following the hearse, the men from the Benevolent Society Death Committee put down the front seats, broke out the schnapps and the cards, and we played poker and joked around.

That was the way Papa wanted it to be, and if I cried, it was because I missed my beautiful Papa, but I was happy he was not in such horrible misery in the hospital.

MAMMA

Mamma was in the Bronx Hospital, and I was working in downtown Manhattan, when I received a telephone call from the hospital. They were angry, said that they needed the bed, that Mamma was a hypochondriac, and she was being discharged right there and then. I left work, ran to the hospital, and up to Mamma's room. It was empty, and when I asked where Mamma was, I got the curt response, Try the morgue. That's where I found Mamma, and I only recognized her because she was still Humpty Dumpty, but she was no longer on her chicken legs.

That's where the young intern found me, and he was crying and said, I loved her—I called her Rosie, you know. She always had a joke and a smile for me. But we couldn't figure out what was wrong because all the tests we performed were negative. Please permit us to perform a postmortem. If you don't then I will drop medicine, because I feel it was all my fault.

I gave him permission to go ahead, and then I had to calm him down and ask what happened in that last half hour.

He said that they had eliminated all physical causes, and called in five psychologists to examine Mamma. There she sat, upright in bed, always with a ribbon in her hair, and telling jokes. The psychologists got pretty angry, and finally one of them poked Rosie and asked, How long would it take you to walk across the Brooklyn Bridge?

Rosie said, Listen, you are about half my age, so why don't you run across, divide by two, and you'll have the answer.

At that point, they all gave up and discharged her. She was dead within five minutes.

And so, Rosie went.

Laurie (By Her Son Marshall)

At the age of eighty, Mom's internal organs were shutting down. We knew the end was near.

Before leaving for the airport to fly home, I spoke with her on the phone. Her voice was calm despite her labored breathing and she remained brave to hide it from me as best she could. Mom was never a complainer. This is not to say she couldn't read you the riot act when she had a mind to.

I begged her to hold on till I made it home and sang her favorite song to her over the phone. It was Irving Berlin's immortal tune, Cheek To Cheek.

Heaven, I'm in heaven
And my heart beats so that I can hardly speak
And I seem to find the happiness I seek
When we're out together dancing cheek to cheek.

I choked up halfway through the song, and begged her again to hold on for me. I then had to ring off to catch my flight.

At the same time, my wife Yelena was by her side, when moments later her doctors came into her room. They told her that she would be moved to a hospice care facility for what remained of her days.

Without hesitation, Mom simply commanded, Pull out the tubes. Pull them all out! Despite Yelena's tearful pleas, The doctor chose to respect Mom's final wish, as I would have done. As with her life, Mom was going to take her own death on her own terms, and that is exactly what she did.

I can only hope that I will find the same courage when my time comes.

Legacy of Love

1. Never interfere between man and wife; when they go to bed you become the enemy.

2. You don't know a man until you've lived with him.

3. Hire a servant and do it yourself.

4. God sits upstairs and pulls the strings downstairs.

5. If it's yours, it walks in the door; if not, you can bang your head against a brick wall.

6. If you hold hands with a boy, you'll have a baby.

7. Listen to everyone's advice; follow your own.

8. Make your own mistakes—not somebody else's.

9. If you don't put it in, you don't take it out.

10. There is enough time to sleep when you are six feet under.

11. It often tickles where you can't scratch.

12. Let evil return from whence it came.

13. How can you guarantee anything if you can't guarantee you'll be alive tomorrow?

14. Gamble with what you can afford to lose; if you win, it is found money,

15. Loan only as much as you can afford to lose; if it is paid back, you are a winner.

16. If you build a bridge, be sure both sides are on firm ground.

17. Look for a cancer, and you'll find a cancer.

18. Don't crap where you eat.

19. A new country, a new name—a change of name is a change of luck.

20. The man who has God in his heart is a good man.

21. God and law are one and the same.

22. For every in there is an out.

23. Every dog has his day, and you're only a puppy.

24. No child of mine is a servant.

25. When your child is born, its life begins and yours ends.

26. Why is efficient bad? Doesn't the sun come up every day? Look at God's handiwork.

27. Children do not add to the number of two, but make a family of one.

28. Before you open your mouth, find out what the other guy knows.

29. Look to people about people; look to books about books.

30. I may not know what I want, but I know what I don't want.

31. You have to be able to afford ideals.

32. Only an ocean can recognize the depth of an ocean; don't be flattered by little brooks.

33. Money lost; nothing lost. Hope lost; all is lost.

34. Always look above you; there will always be plenty below you.

35. No one can hurt you as much as you can hurt yourself.

36. Childhood's laughter provides the strength for the tears of age.

37. Each day you get one day older. So does everyone else.

38. Stay busy building yourself up instead of tearing someone else down.

39. A happy, busy home is seldom spotless.

40. A guest comes for a while and sees for a mile.

41. Only in a poor man's house do you find a little change.

42. It's more important to feed the soul than to feed the stomach.

43. God is a scientist; he never destroyed his mistakes.

44. A friend is like a diamond; an acquaintance is only a rhinestone.

45. If you look good, you feel better.

46. Share the tears, but part on a laugh.

47. Sharpen your teeth on one another; this is how you learn.

48. Play with someone older, from whom you can learn; younger, you teach.

#####

Other Works by Marshall Masters

Godschild Covenant: Return of Nibiru

Gold Fever

Indigo–E.T. Connection

Orange Blossom

Godschild Covenant
Return of Nibiru

Marshall Masters

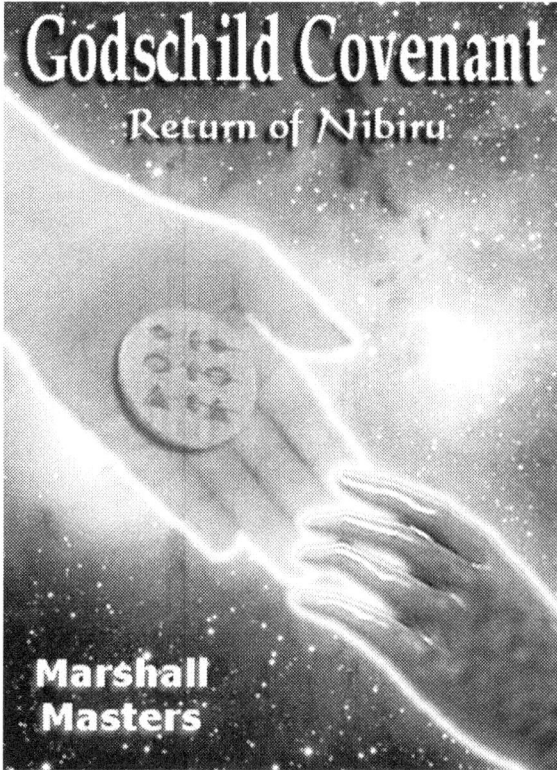

GODSCHILD COVENANT: RETURN OF NIBIRU is a fast-paced action drama set against a global backdrop of tribulation that brings humanity into contact with extraterrestrial races. The story begins in 2011 with the early onset of natural and man-made catastrophes. In the midst of this maelstrom, the pains, secrets, and shady characters of Anthony Jarman's earlier life propel the story at a breathtaking pace, as he struggles to redefine his life through a newfound love for a son he has never met. In the process, he finds himself irresistibly drawn to a dynamic and powerful leader who mourns the recent loss of her own family.

REVIEW: "*Godschild Covenant,* written by Marshall Masters, is a very unique, poetic and uplifting book. In it, Mr. Masters shows great insight into the immense strength of the human spirit, insight which many people alive now have been unable to notice, whether it be because of their busy lifestyle or their aspirations toward a specific goal.

From beginning to end, *Godschild Covenant* demonstrated moving, poetic tenderness. While restricted by circumstances, the story of the sexual love between Anthony and Tanya was shown to be heart wrenching and full of the emotional beauty of a love between two soul mates.

This unique book is futuristic, yet full of truth. It uplifts the reader from the normal, mundane, everyday existence to a place that all of humanity will eventually reach. Ahead of his time, Marshall Masters is giving humanity a message, a prediction, which will soon come to pass. Meanwhile, Marshall, with his mastery of imagination and narrative skill, leads the reader through entertainment to the truth of a realistic, yet hopeful land, the land of the *Godschild Covenant*.

This story surpasses all other novels and works of fiction. It is an immensely rewarding journey; it is so inspiring, so enticing that it makes one want to reach the last word of the book, while still feeling sorry for the fact that the book is drawing to an end." —*Mobipocket's Opinion*

Format	ISBN	DOI
Hardcover	0-9725895-5-4	10.1572/0972589554
Paperback	0-9725895-0-3	10.1572/0972589503
Adobe eBook	0-9725895-1-1	10.1572/0972589511
Microsoft eBook	0-9725895-2-X	10.1572/097258952X
Mobipocket eBook	0-9725895-3-8	10.1572/0972589538
Palm eBook	0-9725895-4-6	10.1572/0972589546

yowbooks.com

Gold Fever

Marshall Masters

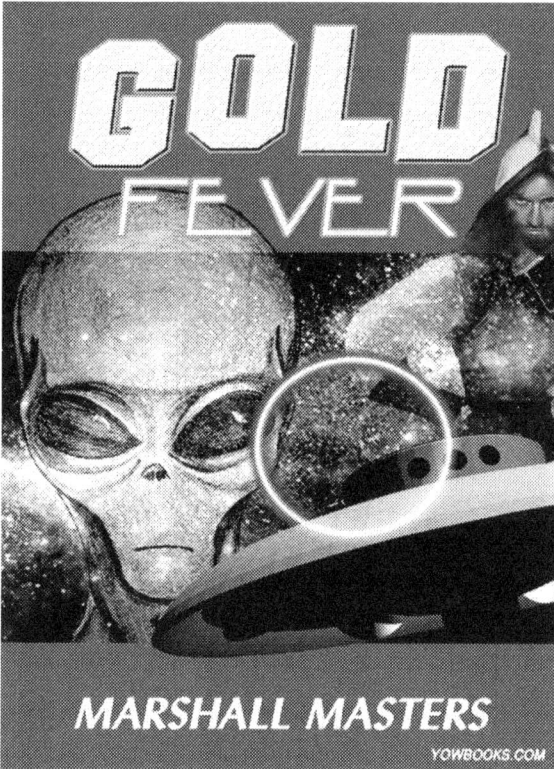

Three adventurous college students set out to find abandoned Spanish gold mines in the hills of Arizona and find unexpected danger and ancient mysteries along the way. The experience not only creates a bond among newfound friends, but also launches a whole new future for humankind.

Format	ISBN	DOI
Adobe eBook	0-9755177-1-6	10.1572/0975517716
Microsoft eBook	0-9755177-0-8	10.1572/0975517708
Mobipocket eBook	0-9755177-7-5	10.1572/0975517775
Palm eBook	1-59772-000-3	10.1572/1597720003

yowbooks.com

Indigo–E.T. Connection

Marshall Masters

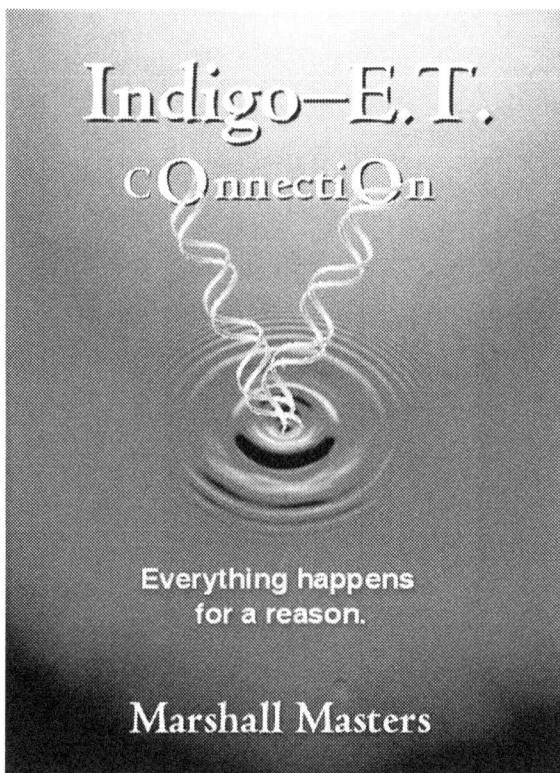

Science tells us that the seeds of life can endure for millennia before a life-nourishing event awakens them. Could this explain the Indigo Child phenomenon? Now, humanity stands upon the cusp of its next evolution, and unprecedented numbers of Indigo Children have awakened to guide the willing towards a brighter future and contact with extraterrestrial races. While some believe that the Indigo Child phenomena began roughly forty years ago, Marshall Masters believes that Indigo Children have always been here and that they are now awakening to the gentle call of a living universe.

REVIEW: "Many researchers are coming to the conclusion that we are not alone in the universe. Not all of these researchers share the same metaphysical commitments, and the trajectories of their works, although roughly parallel, are not exactly the same. But the general conclusion is that we terrestrial humans are part of a whole cosmic hierarchy of beings, with whom we are, have been, or will be in contact in one way or another. Among this group of researchers is Marshall Masters, whose latest book, the Indigo– E.T. Connection, gives his thought provoking ideas on how a small select group of terrestrial humans, with super high IQs and indigo colored auras, may be the best suited for contact with extraterrestrial beings.

For all those interested in the development of the emerging new consensus on the nature of the cosmos, as multidimensional and inhabited by varieties of intelligences, Indigo–E.T. Connection provides a worthwhile contribution to the expanding literature on this topic." —*Michael A. Cremo, Human Devolution, Forbidden Archeology*

Format	ISBN	DOI
Paperback	0-9755177-2-4	10.1572/0975517724
Adobe eBook	0-9755177-3-2	10.1572/0975517732
Microsoft eBook	0-9755177-4-0	10.1572/0975517740
Mobipocket eBook	0-9755177-6-7	10.1572/0975517767
Palm eBook	1-59772-001-1	10.1572/1597720011

yowbooks.com

Orange Blossom

Marshall Masters

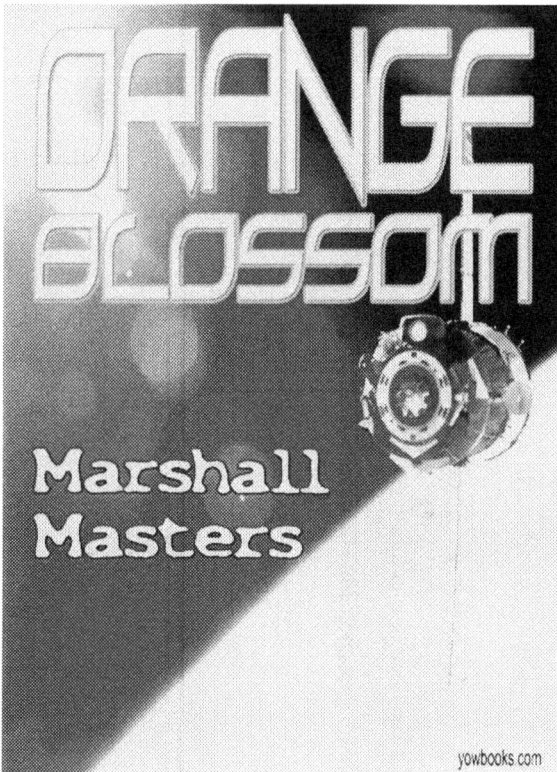

Just when a handsome young aerospace consultant thinks that his contract to document a sophisticated communications satellite system has been mysteriously cut short, he is given an unexpected reprieve. There is a glitch in the ground control system and the brilliant engineer who designed it holds all the answers to his questions-if only he can penetrate her cold and reclusive nature. Tasked to work with him, she persists in keeping both him and his curiosity at arm's length. Though his superiors push him for results, it is the scent of orange blossoms that compel him to uncover the strange glitches in the satellite system as he is drawn towards a life-changing surprise.

Format	ISBN	DOI
Adobe eBook	0-9725895-7-0	10.1572/0972589570
Microsoft eBook	0-9725895-6-2	10.1572/0972589562
Mobipocket eBook	0-9725895-8-9	10.1572/0972589589
Palm eBook	1-59772-002-X	10.1572/159772002X

yowbooks.com

www.ingramcontent.com/pod-product-compliance
Lightning Source LLC
Chambersburg PA
CBHW030026290326
41934CB00005B/510